Experience
the
Impossible

Experience the Impossible

Simple Ways to
Unleash Heaven's Power on Earth

BILL JOHNSON

Chosen

a division of Baker Publishing Group
Minneapolis, Minnesota

© 2014 by Bill Johnson

Published by Chosen Books
11400 Hampshire Avenue South
Bloomington, Minnesota 55438
www.chosenbooks.com

Chosen Books is a division of
Baker Publishing Group, Grand Rapids, Michigan

Printed in the United States of America

Library of Congress Cataloging-in-Publication Data is on file at the Library of Congress, Washington, DC.

ISBN 978-0-8007-9617-4

Scripture quotations are from the New American Standard Bible®, copyright © 1960, 1962, 1963, 1968, 1971, 1972, 1973, 1975, 1977, 1995 by The Lockman Foundation. Used by permission.

Cover design by Dan Pitts

14 15 16 17 18 19 20   7 6 5 4 3 2 1

I dedicate this book to Kris and Kathy Vallotton.

Your love, friendship and partnership
in life and ministry
have made an immeasurable difference
in my life for these past 35+ years.
With great love and affection, thanks.

Contents

Contents

CONTENTS

9

Contents

CONTENTS

Acknowledgments

I want to give special thanks to my personal staff whose tireless service makes so many things possible that would not be otherwise—Michael Van Tinteren, Judy Franklin, Mary Berck and Kezia Neusch.

Introduction

God expects every believer to experience the impossible.
Does that in itself sound impossible? Take heart! It is His
presence upon us that makes the impossible possible. Our job
is to realize, first, that God is truly with us, and, second, that
He wants us to complete every assignment within the Great
Commission for His name and His glory.

Where do we begin? Where is the garden in which we abide
as we grow and bear this Kingdom fruit?

This book of short readings will, I pray, help answer that
question. Based on one of the most well-known and well-loved
verses in the Bible, 1 Corinthians 13:13, we will explore faith,
hope and love. These three aspects of Jesus' grace upon us—and
in us—are the rich earth and rain and sunshine that help us grow
into His likeness and, like Him, unleash heaven's power on earth.

Faith connects us to the power issue. It is faith that enables the
work of God to be done through us effectively. Everyone has
been given a measure of faith. What we do with what we have
determines the extent to which we move in power. *Without faith
we cannot please God.*

Hope is the joyful anticipation of good. It is the place where faith
grows. It is one of the most important attitudes and values—
true Christlikeness. Hope comes from discovering Jesus' perfect

goodness, encountering Him and His perfect promises. *Without hope it is impossible to live life to its potential.*

Love changes everything. Without love we see only hopelessness. Without love we do not have the character to employ faith. Love finds God's promises. Love looks for solutions from a Father who loves perfectly. *Without love we see only law and miss His desire to grace us into victory.*

Each of the 79 entries in this book explores these pivotal topics and ends with a prayer and confession. If we can truly believe that God is with us, we will not only hear His call to walk in Kingdom power, but expect to do so.

Jesus commissioned us to heal the sick, raise the dead and much more. He said that nothing shall be impossible to us. It is time to take the Master at His word, and experience the impossible in His name, for His glory.

1

Faith

Faith does not come from striving; it comes from surrender.

G od is always looking for the sacrifice of the heart, for it is the yielded heart that believes. Faith comes from the heart, not the mind. Living a life of surrender to God can only result in ever-increasing faith. This place of surrender is an expression of dependence on God.

Such dependence comes from humility, which basically means "to see ourselves as He does." Dependence is surrender made manifest. It is what true humility looks like. So, then, faith and humility are related.

Faith is not a product of human intelligence or endeavor. It is not the product of our labors, or it would be of human origin. Faith is otherworldly, firmly anchored in the nature, presence and promises of God. Learning to come before Him in awe, knowing we are accepted by Him, is vital to great faith. Faith is not a product separate from Him, but is instead *because* of Him. Faith is the result of His nature having an impact on the heart of the believer.

The priests of the Old Testament could not wear wool in God's presence as wool might have made them sweat. They were instructed to wear linen. The picture is fairly clear—we cannot come before God through our own labors (sweat). We must come before Him through His labors, which were designed to make us acceptable before Him.

Faith is called both a fruit and a gift of the Spirit. You have never heard a fruit tree groan and travail to produce fruit. Growing fruit is the evidence that the tree is holding its place (abiding) in the soil in order to receive nutrients, sunlight and moisture correctly. In the same way, those who abide in Christ cannot help but grow in faith as the result of being continually exposed to His nature through His Word and His manifest presence. It is as natural a result as it is for an apple tree to produce apples.

When I find that I am anxious, I ask myself the all-important question, Where did I lose my peace? If I can answer that one, I am usually able to spot the lie I believed that brought about such conflict in my soul. Confession and forsaking sin follow, which is what God uses to restore peace. And that place of peace is the place where faith matures.

Prayer

Father, I acknowledge that Jesus made it possible for me to come before You. This privilege was not something I could have earned. So I rest in the accomplishments of Jesus on my behalf. I also recognize that in my surrender to You, Your heart becomes manifest through me. And that is my great desire. Be glorified in and through me this day!

Confession

I choose to live a surrendered life today, believing that God will be glorified in who I am and all I do. I live this way because I am highly favored of the Lord. His peace—the atmosphere of heaven—is my portion.

2

Hope

The presence of the Lord upon us positions us for miracles.

Many times throughout the Bible, the Lord spoke to His servants saying He would be with them. Sometimes He even described it this way: "The Spirit of the Lord came upon them." I once made a list of every such encounter recorded in Scripture. I found an interesting truth: Whenever the Lord said He would be with someone, it meant he had just been given an impossible assignment.

God gave such a promise to Moses. It was connected to his assignment to lead Israel out of Egypt and out of the cruel control of Pharaoh into the Promised Land. A similar word was given to Joshua, the one who took over when Moses was not allowed into the Promised Land. Joshua was assigned to lead them into their inheritance, in spite of giants and other fearful enemies. The same promise was given to Gideon, who was then to deliver a weak and humiliated Israel from the powerfully oppressive hand of the Midianites. And again the same was given to the eleven remaining disciples in the Great Commission in Matthew 28. It was tied to their assignment to *disciple nations.* The implications of the promised presence are staggering. God's presence requires something from us—the invasion into the impossible.

Something is always expected *from us* when God is revealed to be *with us.* It is a grave mistake to think the Holy Spirit is among us simply to comfort or encourage. That is a given. He is also present to make possible the impossible task in front of us! Perhaps this is part of what the apostle Paul wanted us to see when he asked God to show us the hope of our calling (see Ephesians 1:18–19).

One of my favorite verses, one that has had the most impact on me, has to do with Jesus, the eternal Son of God:

> "You know of Jesus of Nazareth, how God anointed Him with the Holy Spirit and with power, and how He went about doing good and healing all who were oppressed by the devil, for God was with Him."
>
> Acts 10:38

This verse gives us a synopsis of what is already revealed throughout the gospels: Jesus healed and delivered all who came to Him. It also reveals that sickness is from the devil. But the Holy Spirit wanted to make sure we know what made healing and deliverance possible: "For God was with Him." Although Jesus is eternally God, and never stopped being God, the Holy Spirit inspired Luke to pen this phrase, *for God was with Him.* This statement shows us that it was the same for Jesus as it was for our heroes in the Old Testament. When God is with someone, he is expected and enabled to invade the impossible. This helps us to connect with our God-given assignment by realizing and discovering His presence upon us, which makes the impossible possible.

Often when I see 10:38 on a clock, I stop and direct my heart to God and give Him thanks for the revelation of the nature and promise of God found in the life of Jesus. Interestingly, while writing on this quote, I looked at the clock on my phone, and it is 10:38. I am thankful for this Scripture that will ignite the hearts of many to invade the impossible in His name and for His glory—for God is truly with us!

Jesus started His ministry with a bold confession: "The Spirit of the Lord is upon Me, because He anointed Me to . . ." (Luke 4:18). The confession that started His ministry also revealed the nature of His ministry. It was to bring freedom to people, and it was because of the presence of the Spirit of God upon Him.

Prayer

Help me to become more aware of Your presence upon me as the hope of my calling into the impossible. Help me to see my assignment as being impossible, so that I do not become confident in my abilities instead of Yours. Let this be a day of great breakthrough as I discover the wonder of being the temple of the Holy Spirit.

Confession

The Spirit of the Lord God is upon me for the same reason He rested upon Jesus. I embrace the call to the impossible, that God may be glorified in all the earth.

3

Love

The same Spirit that raised Jesus from
the dead is in you, and He wants out.

The metaphoric picture Jesus gave in John 7:38 of the indwelling Spirit of God is that of a river. Rivers start somewhere and go somewhere. In this case, the Spirit of the resurrected Christ starts with God Himself, who dwells in us and is to flow out of us, touching the world around us. He is in us as a river, not a lake. He is constantly moving.

In Matthew 10:8, Jesus told His disciples that they had something to give, by commanding them, "Freely you received; freely give." Love requires giving. "For God so loved the world, that He gave . . ." (John 3:16). While I believe He is primarily referring to releasing the Holy Spirit, the lesson could apply to anything He has given us, which would include things like favor, mercy, love, time and money. The list is endless, really. He gives to us hoping we will give to another. The way His life is to increase on the earth is by those He has favored to release it to others. Interestingly, we get to keep only what we give away.

This picture is basically saying that we release, or give the Spirit of God away, in our activities as believers. If that is true, then it would do us well to consider His nature and passions.

He cooperates with those who carry His heart. Compassion is a huge part of expressing the heart of God. It is not sympathy; nor is it merely identifying with a person who has an issue. Sympathy locks a person in a problem, while compassion pulls him or her out. Sympathy supports a person's identity being built around his problem, such as a disease, like *blind Bartimaeus*. Compassion sees what can be and pulls it into the now.

This metaphor of the Holy Spirit as a river illustrates our lives as a flow of something. This "flow" happens as we love people. The power of God is expressed or released from us in all life and ministry that is truly pleasing to Him. Every time we minister in His name, declaring His truth, serving with His heart and demonstrating His power, there is a flow that goes forth from us. While this concept may be a bit abstract for the Western rational culture, it is still very much Kingdom. All life and ministry that is pleasing to Him is actually a release of His presence into a situation.

We know instinctively that self-centered living does little to release the presence of God into a situation. We would never, for example, expect the shadow of a depressed follower of Jesus to heal anyone. Why? Because, like it or not, we all release the nature of the world we are most aware of into the world around us. A depressed believer is not focused on God's abiding presence, His Kingdom or His promises. That is why depression has such a deep-seated control over her mind and emotions, bringing a cloud over her spirit. But the one abiding in Christ, with His words filling her heart, can expect the same outcome as found in the Scriptures. The atmosphere around her changes according to the atmosphere within her. This is the great impact of the Gospel lived in community. That is why the Kingdom is called leaven. It works subtly through all who give Him place in their hearts.

Realizing this truth enables us to live more intentionally. When we live aware of the Spirit of God in us, we are much more inclined to realize when His presence is released from us. Discovering the nature of the mysterious is one of the great joys of following the One whose name is Truth.

Prayer

I need Your help to live aware of You above all else. So many things compete for my attention, and, therefore, my affection, that I find it difficult at times to live consistently aware of Your Spirit within me. But that is truly what I long for. Help me in this next season to grow in my confidence in Your abiding presence, and to give love the way You do. Thank You for the Spirit without measure.

Confession

I confess with the psalmist, "One thing I have asked from the LORD, that I shall seek" (Psalm 27:4). I will forever delight in the Holy Spirit, the gift sent to me from Jesus Himself, and seek for the increased manifestation of this indescribable One. I was born for this purpose, to know and manifest this glorious One to those I know and love.

4

Faith

Regardless of the level of faith, Jesus always brought a miracle.

Faith is anchored in His Word. The credibility of His Word is linked to His nature. To know Him, we need to encounter Him and experience His nature. One of the ways people experience Him in Scripture is through miracles, signs and wonders.

Jesus often addressed the issue of faith by exposing unbelief and then exhorting people to believe. Yet He never withheld a miracle because of faith in small measure. He healed everyone who came to Him, regardless of the person's heart condition. When Jesus addressed small faith, it was never to humiliate or condemn. It was always to position the person to grow in faith, for without faith we cannot please God. Miracles made people more aware of their divine moments and ensured that they responded to God with greater trust—which is greater faith, the result of what they just experienced.

I have been unable to find a smaller measure of faith than that in the heart of the father with the child who needed healing and deliverance, whose story is told in Mark 9. This compassionate but overwhelmed father had seen the demons try to kill his child while he stood by helpless. What made matters worse was that he had brought the child to the disciples, but they could not help.

The father said to Jesus/God, "If You can do anything . . ." (Mark 9:22). Imagine the kind of faith that is not even sure God is capable. His desperate cry moved the heart of Jesus. But before Jesus performed the requested miracle, He turned the tables on him by saying, "'If You can?' All things are possible to him who believes" (verse 23). In other words, God's ability to perform a miracle is not in question. The only question that remains is, Will you believe? This story is where the well-known quote comes from: *I believe, but help me in my unbelief.*

Most of us read our Bibles with religious, cultural biases more than we realize. Look at this verse, for example. Jesus said, "Unless you people see signs and wonders, you simply will not believe" (John 4:48). I grew up imagining that His tone of voice was one of disgust because He was scolding them for the weak faith that must have some kind of experience in order to believe. But what if He was just acknowledging how faith grows? That thought seems to be supported by the fact that Jesus followed this statement with a miracle. Why? First of all, miracles always came out of His love for people. But secondly, He wanted them to grow in faith. And He had just the process for their development—seeing signs and wonders.

Jesus used what little measure this father had, and then positioned him for increase by drawing his attention to God's heart, nature and purpose. Miracles always put people in a position to increase. The entire New Testament confirms this fact. What people do in response to what God does is up to them. But the process is clear—people believe because of miracles.

Faith is vital. It is through faith we please God; faith is that essential. But to shift our focus to our measure of faith alone is to ignore that Jesus never punished people who knew whom to come to, even if they had small faith. Whenever we concern ourselves only with a particular measure of faith, we have turned our focus from God and His nature seen in His promises, to ourselves and what we carry. That is always a dead-end road.

Prayer

Heavenly Father, Your goodness and kindness are beyond my comprehension. I love You so much for always going past my expectations. Please help me to stop evaluating how well I am doing; instead, help me to be caught up with who You are and what You are like. I come to You as I am, with blemishes and weakness included. And I thank You in advance that You will complete the good work You have started in me.

Confession

I confess that God's goodness is not restricted by my faith, and that God has chosen to use the weak things to confound the wise. I am designed to believe God. That is my nature.

5

Hope

It is illegal to enjoy the presence of the Lord and not conquer something.

When Isaiah was before the Lord, beholding Him upon His throne, he was overwhelmed by what he saw. He beheld things that were beyond description. He then heard the Lord ask a question: "Whom shall I send?" Isaiah responded, "I'll go, send me."

Worship is the ultimate ministry. But I run into people often who consider themselves to be great worshipers, but do nothing else outside of that activity. I question the experience of anyone who says he has encountered the Lord, but is not willing to serve. What authenticated Isaiah's experience in the throne room was the quickness with which he volunteered to answer God's search for a willing vessel. It is nearly impossible to see His heart and then turn a cold shoulder to His search for a volunteer.

I believe in the beauty of worship. In fact, it is *the great privilege* for the believer to be invited into the throne room of God to minister unto Him. It is not to be taken lightly. But to minister to Him and not serve shows that in our worship we have not seen or encountered His heart. It is easy in a worshiping culture to lose focus and actually worship *worship*—that is to love the music, the atmosphere, the joy of being together as the people of God, but never actually encounter the face of God. It would be like enjoying the party of a wealthy friend. Your friends are there, there is great food, great music and a very enjoyable atmosphere in the room. You look across the room and acknowledge the host, but never go over to him, never even express your thanks for the event, his kindness and who he is in your life. It is easy to enjoy the benefits of our Friend, but seldom actually encounter Him.

All who consider themselves abandoned worshipers of God must ask themselves this question: Is my passion for His presence measureable outside of the expression of worship? If not, changes must be made. Jesus did not do all He did so we would do nothing. Our love for God is measured by our love for people. The unseen realities in our lives (our love for God) must be measurable in the seen (our love for people). Our lives have the hope of eternal impact. Jesus made this possible, and probable.

Great love for God looks for ways to display His love by opposing or hating the things He hates, namely those things that seek to kill, steal and destroy people's lives. This is the honored assignment given to Jesus by the Father and passed on to us in the Great Commission. One of Jesus' final statements of commission was given in John 20:21: "As the Father has sent Me, I also send you." Lovers of God have the privilege of enforcing the victory won at the cross against all the enemies of humanity. This, in fact, is a part of our worship expression.

The Spirit of God who comes upon us in a unique way during worship longs to be seen through us outside of our work, devotion or worship expressions. Worship truly comes full circle when we embrace His heart for people and work to see His name exalted through the victories afforded to us by the redemptive work of Jesus.

Prayer

Thank You for giving me the privilege of entering Your throne room as a worshiper. Please help me never to lose sight of why I was given this great privilege. I also ask that You help me always to connect with Your heartbeat that I may always carry Your passion for people.

Confession

I have been favored of the Lord to come before His face in worship. Because of this favor, I have the hope to be able to express His heart wherever I go, that He may be exalted in the earth.

6

Love

It is hard to have the same fruit as
the early Church when we value a
book they did not have more than
the Holy Spirit they did have.

F̲ew statements I make cause as much grief as this one. And
I understand why. In reading between the lines one could
think I do not value, or have little value for, the Scriptures. Some
accuse me of trying to devalue the place the Bible has in our
lives. Nothing could be further from the truth. If that were the
case, the strong reactions would be deserved. But it is not the
case—and neither is it what was stated. We must maintain the
value of Scripture, while increasing our value of the Holy Spirit.
It is not either/or. It is both/and. If we truly love God, that love
must have expression toward the Holy Spirit, too.

We are privileged to have the complete canon of Scripture—
the Bible. So many people in history paid the ultimate price
to make that possible. *I love the Bible!* I am constantly *in the
Word*, as many would put it. And I am constantly working to
get that Word into me. This process is one of my greatest joys
and treasures. But the point remains: *It is hard to have the same*

fruit as the early Church when we value a book they did not have more than the Holy Spirit they did have.

Jack Taylor addresses the issue this way: "It's not Father, Son and Holy Bible!" He states it well. For many, the Bible has taken the place of the Holy Spirit. And He is the author! *It* is not to replace the *He*. There is potentially a brilliant partnership of heaven and earth when we learn how to listen to, and work with, the Holy Spirit in our study of Scripture, and in our living out the biblical mandate to live as Jesus lived—invading the impossible.

The fear ultimately is that we will emphasize experience over and above Scripture. Such concern is legitimate. Great errors have entered the Church during those seasons. But the opposite is a much more common, and an even greater error: It is *faith without experience*. Some have made this a virtue. And anything we label a virtue has permission to stay, no matter how inconsistent with biblical standards it might be. It becomes the new norm. As a result, those without experience begin defining what the Bible says.

We would never let someone without the experience of being born again teach what it means to be born again. Teaching out of experience is not only acceptable; it is necessary. It is only when experience contradicts Scripture that we must be concerned.

We are much more privileged than the early Church because we have the completed canon of Scripture readily available. This wonderful gift—the written Word of God—gives us an advantage that the early Church did not have. Yet, if in their lack they *turned the world upside down*, then we are without excuse. For we have the Bible, and the Author lives inside us! It was the Person of the Holy Spirit who empowered them, directed them, gave them understanding of what they were to do with what they were facing. He spoke life into every part of their lives, for He was their life. This great gift of heaven made it possible for them to illustrate the life of Jesus accurately not only in character and compassion but also in miracles, signs and wonders. This passionate love for God must now be demonstrated toward the One who inspired the book—God's Word.

Do not listen to anyone who devalues the written Word of God. But also be careful around anyone who does not model a life of tenderness toward the Holy Spirit. The Word and the Spirit give us the great advantage. Perhaps this is why Scripture says, "The latter glory of this house will be greater than the former" (Haggai 2:9).

Prayer

Father, let this day be a day of increased awareness and fellowship with the great treasure of heaven—the Holy Spirit. I want to celebrate Him as You do. And I want to live by His power, fulfilling the commission given in Scripture. I long for the Spirit of wisdom and revelation to rest upon me that I might learn continuously what is written in Your Word. Let this day truly be for the glory of God.

Confession

I declare that I was born for this purpose, and am thoroughly equipped to face this day living in partnership with heaven and earth. I embrace, with great joy, the privilege of being the dwelling place of the Holy Spirit.

7

Faith

Faith is what sticks to us
from encountering the
"faith-fullness" of God.

Every person has been given a measure of faith. When that faith is used to enjoy God and His wonders, our confidence in Him increases. Well-stewarded faith increases faith itself.

Worship is one of the most profound activities for the believer in that change happens with us simply because of the effect of His presence upon us. Giving God praise, as an expression of faith, gives us access to the *more of God*.

He is faithful, perfectly faithful. Encountering the One who is faithful draws us into a relationship of trust and risk. Seeing the One who is perfectly faithful does something to us. Imagine hugging someone who is wearing way too much cologne. You walk away carrying the scent of her cologne. Similarly, drawing near to the One who is faithful results in my increase of faith. To describe it more literally, who He is sticks to me by leaving its mark on my heart and mind. Faith is really nothing more or less than being confident in who He is. The result is increased faith. When we encounter Him, we discover who He is and what He is like. Faith is anchored in His nature and character.

34

This pattern is seen in the lives of those known for their great faith. They discovered through experience what many already knew in their theology, that God is true to His Word. Such faithfulness is His cologne, so to speak. Faithfulness on Him becomes faith on us—faith is the residue. Many make the mistake of trying to grow their faith through striving and self-determination. This always leads to disappointment and frustration. It can also lead to presumption, which is counterfeit faith—and devastating. Use the measure of faith you have to discover Him for the sake of knowing Him. Increased faith is the result.

Prayer

Father, help me to discover the unending treasure of Your faithfulness in this next season. I choose to place my attention on who You are, and will resist the temptation to focus on my level of faith. Please let this be unto the glory of God!

Confession

I serve the One who is faithful and true. He cannot lie. This will be a day of great discovery of who He is, beyond all I could imagine or think. He is the joy of my life! I am a believing believer, who lives to bring Him glory.

8

Hope

Jesus did not perform miracles to show us what God can do.

The amazing displays of power and glory in the Old Testament already gave a brief glimpse of the wonders that God is capable of performing. Creation of the world by the spoken word certainly sets a high-water mark for signs that make one wonder. Jesus came to reveal something else, something quite unexpected. He came to reveal what *one man* could do who was rightly related to God. This revelation is meant to create hope for a purpose-filled life.

Jesus Christ is God, eternally God. Never in His earthly existence did He take a vacation from His divinity. In other words, He is and was always God. But His earthly life was equally natural in that He was also fully man. The very fact that angels came to strengthen Him testifies to this fact, as God would not need such strengthening. This is one of the great mysteries of all eternity. Jesus was fully God and fully man. But Jesus spoke of Himself as the Son of Man. He lived as the Son of Man.

This point is absolutely essential for us to understand, because it affects the way we live. If Jesus did miracles of healing, deliverance, multiplying food and raising the dead as God, I am still impressed—but it is not something I can duplicate. I am a spectator, which I am very happy about if that is my divine assignment. But when I realize that He did what He did as a man yielded to God, then I am compelled to follow, discovering that is my real assignment! And I might never do well the things He did. But I am unable to stay where I am because Jesus set a standard for life that can be followed and imitated.

There were two things that made His humanity supernaturally effective: He was without sin, and He lived completely under the empowerment of the Holy Spirit. Those two qualifications—our righteousness in Christ and our living empowered by the Holy Spirit—become the necessary ingredients for every man, woman and child alive who longs to accept the compelling invitation that Jesus' life gives. "Follow Me" now takes on new meaning.

Jesus did not go through all His sufferings so we could go to church; He did what He did to atone for sin. And by doing so He made it possible to raise up a new breed of world changers, those who could maintain the standard He set in love, purity and power. This reality is one of the great prophecies that Jesus spoke: "Greater works than these shall you do because I go to the Father" (see John 14:12). Not only does Jesus' life compel us to follow the miracle worker, so do His promises.

The blood of Jesus, then, qualifies us for the first part of this equation. As a forgiven son, I am justified, cleansed, washed clean. This is a greater reality than my sinful past. I now stand before the Father, in Christ. He sees me as He sees His Son, Jesus. So only one qualification remains. How much under the influence of the Holy Spirit am I willing to live?

Prayer

Father God, I give myself to You in a fresh way today. I want to represent Jesus accurately. Thank You for the blood of Your Son that makes me free from sin and qualifies me for the impossible. I am so hungry to see the authentic Gospel lived more fully in and through my life. I invite the Holy Spirit to come upon me more and more until Jesus is what people see when they look at me. Make this dream a reality for Your glory!

Confession

I declare that I was created to be part of the "greater works" generation. I embrace this call of God upon my life, that the name of Jesus might be held in highest honor all over the earth!

9

Love

A powerless Church has little for the devil to counterfeit.

In some Christian circles, the Good News of miracles and transformed lives does not bring excitement; it brings warning. God has been absent so long that when something powerful happens, they think it is the devil. Thus, any of us who see a miracle and declare the Good News to others often receive a pile of warnings in return about the possibility of false signs and wonders. That is a legitimate concern, as the Bible warns against them, too. But we need to remember that there has to be something real to counterfeit, as the devil is not a creator. He has no creative ability whatsoever. Instead, he is a distorter of what already exists. The very fact that the Bible warns against false signs and wonders and false prophets implies there are real ones to compare them to.

Much of the Church lives with little or no power. Believers sit comfortably with the notion that they are okay because they do not face spiritual opposition. But if I do not run into the devil now and then, I might be going the same direction.

It is true that a legally parked car breaks no laws. But this *car* was designed to go places and accomplish things. The fear of making mistakes and not doing a particular ministry well has paralyzed many believers, and that is a tragedy. They fail to see that perfectionism is religion (form without power). Excellence is Kingdom. Saying yes to the King is the first step in discipleship. And being driven by love makes it impossible to remain stationary.

One of our greatest honors in life is to represent Jesus accurately. This is done through love, purity and power. Often what we value here on earth has little value in heaven. Believers, for example, often place their highest value on a church without mistakes (the legally parked car). Heaven values a church that has impact.

People in banking systems are trained to spot counterfeit money. Their training, however, has nothing to do with counterfeit money. They spend enormous amounts of time studying the real so that the fake becomes obvious. Counterfeit miracles become easier to spot when you live in the midst of the real. False prophets stand out in a crowd of real prophets.

Many think that a false prophet is uncovered when a prophetic word is inaccurate, but that is not necessarily true. Study the prophecies of Agabus in the book of Acts. He was a true prophet of God, as acknowledged by the Holy Spirit, but not all the details of his word to Paul were accurate. For this reason, the believer is given the assignment to judge the word, not the prophet. The false prophet and false miracle worker are easy to spot among real because the "supernatural realm" they walk in directs the attention of the followers to themselves and not the Lord. They live to build their own kingdoms, have their own followers and entice people to live for them.

Prayer

Heavenly Father, help me to represent Jesus well today. I commit myself to His standard of love, purity and power. Let these realities be increasingly evident in and through my life, all for the glory of God.

Confession

I declare that I was born for this purpose, and that it has already been decided that I should carry Jesus' presence and purpose to the world around me. I will demonstrate His love daily, and give Him thanks in advance for what is about to take place! I do all of this for the glory of God.

10

Faith

The walk of faith is to live
according to the revelation we
have received, in the midst of
mysteries we cannot explain.

I love revelation. It was important enough for Paul to pray for
the church at Ephesus to receive it. I love it when God opens
our hearts to see things that we could not see without His help.
One of the greatest experiences in life is when God opens His
Word to an individual. Seeing from His perspective changes
everything, starting with us. But as important as understanding
is to the life of a believer, mystery is also important. In fact, it
is as important as revelation. Putting it another way, *what I do
not know is as important as what I do know.*

The realm of mystery defines how my trust in God is lived out
on a day-to-day basis. Living joyfully in the midst of mystery
is evidence of great faith, and as such is required territory for
every believer longing to grow in Christ. Perhaps this is why this
Gospel is called "the faith" and not "the understanding." It is
in our new nature to believe God.

There are those who object to putting too much value
on mystery, reminding us of the biblical mandate to pursue

understanding. They are correct, as such a pursuit is clearly laid out in Scripture for every follower of Jesus. It is especially emphasized in the book of Proverbs and lived out by the disciples of Jesus. While that is absolutely true, there must also be a victorious, heartfelt response that we give to Him *in the meantime* until He answers the questions of our heart. That is the great strength of faith. It stands when reasoning falls.

The real issue at hand is obedience. Understanding is not needed for obedience; faith is. If I obey only when I understand, I have reduced God to my size, someone who always has to explain Himself before I respond. That is a dangerous posture for true believers as we have been called into lives of abandonment and absolute trust. While such a position may be considered wisdom, it is actually the sign of great immaturity in that it depends on human reasoning.

Someone being healed of cancer has become reasonable. It is becoming the new norm. A believer dying of cancer is a mystery, one I do not understand. What I do understand is God's goodness. I do understand that the payment for our healing has been paid in full out of that goodness. And I will not sacrifice my understanding of the nature of God on the altar of human reasoning so that I have an explanation for cancer taking someone's life. Cancer is wrong. It does not exist in heaven, and it cannot be okay that is exists here on earth. That would violate our assignment in the Lord's Prayer. And I must give myself to seeing the name of the Lord vindicated from the casual acceptance of cancer and other afflictions as things that God uses to make us stronger people. Jesus never used that approach to the sick. We must follow His lead.

Prayer

Father, I long for understanding of Your Word, Your nature and Your heart for me. I acknowledge that You are good. You are better than I could ever have hoped for. My cry is that You will give me grace to cling to You in the midst of mystery so I do not falter in my confidence in You. Help me to live according to what You have shown me without stumbling over the things that remain a mystery. I always want to represent You well by manifesting Your goodness to the people I am privileged to serve.

Confession

I will declare God's goodness when things look good and especially when they do not. My God never changes. I confess His great promise to turn every situation around for His glory and for my benefit. He is a perfectly wonderful Father, one I delight in celebrating!

11

Hope

Every loss is temporary;
every victory is eternal.

One of the great mysteries in life is that bad things do happen to good people. There are losses and setbacks, even for believing believers. One need only look at the apostle Paul's life to figure that one out—shipwrecks, beatings, hunger, lies, opposition in every city, etc. Yet the march is onward and upward toward the call and purposes of God for our lives. We are not defined by our circumstances. This is the overriding hope for every follower of Jesus. Such moments are reminders that we are not perfect, but are instead being perfected.

We have noted that some make the mistake of assuming that God sent a bad situation in order to make us stronger believers. His ability to turn a dark situation around has caused some to credit Him with the problem in the first place. That is an unhealthy leap in logic, as that kind of reasoning has God creating evil so He can display His goodness. That would be like a parent beating a child so he could love and comfort her. Evil exists apart from God. For many of us, our understanding of His sovereignty must change.

Unbelief and the lack of passion cause many to give way to dark circumstances, assuming God sent them. Yet if it is a health issue, the same people will go to a doctor to have him or her fix what they say God sent their way. It is normal to fight against evil. Our reasoning must become biblical and catch up to what we know instinctively is right.

Eternity is the cornerstone of logic and reason. Without that simple anchor of the soul, the river of ideas and lifestyles runs without banks. Tragically, many function without any purpose or sense of accountability. Living with the realization that we will give an account of our lives adds a measure of wisdom that cannot be reached any other way. With that in mind, consider this: Eternity puts loss in its place. Losses are temporary. Every setback and defeat is put in its place because of eternity. And then add to that the realization that the work of the Redeemer takes every bad situation and works it for our good. So not only is every loss temporary, it is actually reversed in its effect to become a blessing and even grounds for personal promotion and gain. And all of that pertains to loss. This is why every believer is able to live with constant hope. Not even wrong things have the ability to derail us.

Every positive thing that happens to us is a building block for our eternal purpose, as this life is school for eternity. We are being trained to rule and reign with Christ. We will not be sitting on a cloud, playing harps. God is a God of continual advancement. The Bride will be adorned beautifully for His glory. And she will come into the fullness of what He has planned for her. It is one of those things that we probably would not believe if it were told to us. It is beyond our wildest dreams. This life is the preparation for that role.

Victories reveal eternal purpose by unveiling God's system of rewards. Some say they are not interested in rewards; they just want to know God. As noble as it sounds, it seriously undermines God's economy of faith. Faith requires us to believe He is, and that "He is a rewarder of those who seek Him" (Hebrews 11:6).

All of our victories are a part of our stories—our testimonies. These testimonies will be treasured for all eternity, as each one is a building block of our stories. We will know one another as we are known and will see one another's story. We will stand in awe and give praise over and over again to the One who works such wonders in people's lives. We will finally catch a glimpse of the wonderful tapestry called the history of humanity.

Victories are forever, as they give us a foretaste of heaven, and train us for eternity.

Prayer

Father, please help me to keep Your perspective on my losses. And help me to realize that all these things work for good because You are good, and You are God. Also increase my understanding of my eternal purpose, as I do not want to live ignorant of the things You are making available to us.

Confession

I declare that God makes everything work for His glory, and for my good. I commit to Him all my weakness, failures, triumphs and successes that He might be glorified!

12

Love

The *heart* to hear God's voice
is much more important than
the *ability* to hear His voice.

Eric, my oldest son, is profoundly deaf. He is the senior leader of our local church and has an amazing teaching gift and miracle anointing. Together we have seen hundreds of miracles pertaining to deafness. It has been wonderful. But he has not been healed—yet.

He wears a hearing aid in one ear, and is unable to wear one in the other. His hearing loss is in the 85 to 90 percent range, so you can imagine how this affects his life. Yet his ability to function normally is an amazing gift of grace from God. It is astounding to all who know the facts.

I have never required him to hear me better. I never speak softly and then get angry at him for not hearing. It is my responsibility to be heard. Love requires that I adjust my actions to meet his abilities. Sometimes that means that I speak louder than I would to somebody else. If it is a noisy room, I will make sure he is looking at me so that seeing my lips will reinforce what he is hearing.

All of us hear God's voice. We could not be saved otherwise. He called us to Himself, and we responded and became born again. That is the only way conversion happens. Jesus described our God-given ability when He said that His sheep know His voice. It is a divinely given grace to hear God's voice. But many believers are more aware of how bad their hearing is as they compare themselves to someone they admire. And while that might be true, it is destructive in nature. The *heart* to hear is more important than our *ability* to hear. The reason? God takes the responsibility to be heard whenever He finds someone who desires to hear. Sometimes we need to get out of the noisy room, so to speak. In other words, take time quietly to seek God with the Scriptures in hand. Giving thanks and enjoying His presence (face) is a beautiful way to activate our ability to hear, be it weak or strong. Encountering His face does a lot to help us *read His lips.* Hearing Him speak through the Scriptures does a lot to help me hear Him speak to my heart.

James 1:21 describes this process in a beautiful way: "In humility receive the word implanted, which is able to save your souls." Humility is the condition of the soil that receives the Word. Another way to say this is: Humility is the heart condition that attracts God's voice into your situation. And when God speaks, He plants the answer into the tender hearts of His children. The seed is the Word. The Word carries the ability to save us. In other words, His Word has the ability to perform itself in and through our hearts. Humble hearts hear well.

Prayer

Father God, please help me to stay away from the trap of evaluating my ability to hear over and above Your ability to be heard. Instead I turn my attention to how much You love me! I want to keep my focus on You, not on my abilities, be they great or small. I do want to increase in my ability to hear Your voice. But more than anything, I ask You to help me maintain a humble heart so that You can always find a place to plant the seeds of hope and promise. I thank You in advance for helping me to be all that You created me to be—a hearer of the voice of God.

Confession

I was created with the ability to hear God's voice. That ability is in my new nature given to me in Christ. And even in my weakness, He is strong and is more than capable of speaking loudly enough for me to hear Him. I set my heart to be a hearer of His voice, as I know that I live by every Word that proceeds from His mouth. And I declare that, as a hearer of His voice, I will do all He says I will do.

13

Faith

If you live cautiously, your friends
will call you wise. You just won't
move many mountains.

While there is a caution born out of wisdom, our challenge is to spot the counterfeit—whatever comes from the fear of man. This kind of fear is an affliction of the heart. It causes us to silence courage by wondering what someone will think of us if we make a bold move. I believe this single issue has caused more stunted growth in the people of God than any other issue.

The cautious ones are often known for their discipline and Bible study. They are usually good teachers of the principles of God's Word, and are quiet outside of their public responsibilities, should they have any. These traits can all be valuable. But such a person seldom has an effect on his mountain, so to speak. He is much more likely to teach us how to live with and endure our mountains. In this context, timidity gets called anything but what it is. It is fear. A quiet spirit is Kingdom; timidity is not.

History is filled with the stories of brave men and women of God who broke out of the acceptable norm only to raise the bar on what was considered to be the normal Christian life.

Their breakthroughs changed how we do life, and even more importantly, what we can expect to take place through our lives. But they paid a price. Today they are the heroes of the faith. But in their day, they were often rejected and maligned by their peers. Many of them died lonely and despised by the church. As tragic as that is, it reveals an issue that everyone faces in measure, but not everyone is willing to embrace as a challenge—we must demonstrate the life of Christ in the full measure of love, purity and power, regardless of the cost.

Smith Wigglesworth was such a man. My mom's side of the family was greatly impacted by his ministry. My grandfather once told me that not everyone liked Wigglesworth. Of course, he is highly respected today as the legendary apostle of faith. But that is because he is dead. Israel did the same with her prophets: They were rejected in their day only to be revered once they had died. It is easy to admire accomplishments from a distance (either geographical, or in time). It is quite another to endure and respect those whose passion is to pursue living an authentic Gospel in ways that challenge our comfort zones. Such is the nature of real faith. It offends the stationary.

Faith is not seen in foolishness; nor does it attract attention to itself. It does not need to prove itself, as that usually ends in disappointment. Faith is focused entirely on God and exists because of Him. Faith is active, and is completely dissatisfied with theories and ideals that cannot be proven, that do not bear fruit. It derives its life from the voice and nature of God. It is unto God, to bring Him pleasure and glory. Such a life is anything but a comfortable life of caution. It is bold, brave, courageous and risky.

Prayer

Father, I want my life to count for something. For that to happen, You must pour great grace upon me. I confess that I have feared what others might think of me at the expense of considering what You value. Forgive me. I am tired of living with mountains that are outside of Your purposes. Forgive me for giving them virtuous names that have allowed them to remain. By Your grace I will be bold and declare who You are without shame or fear.

Confession

By my nature in Christ I am bold and filled with faith. I will fear no man, but fear God only, and love not my life unto death. I embrace this as the privilege of every follower of Jesus. And let mountains be removed now for the glory of God!

14

Hope

I pay no attention to the warnings
of possible excess from those
who are satisfied with lack.

The most exciting time in the life of the Church is when the
Holy Spirit begins to move in power. So many things happen
outside of the usual experience that to say it is *a learning season*
is a huge understatement. And so the education begins—great
change is in the air.

In the middle of miracles and changed lives is the group that
always questions what is happening. That is not necessarily a
bad thing—not if humility and hunger accompany the questions
and the subsequent journey. In fact, none of us responds to the
Holy Spirit's moving in the same way; nor do we accept it in
the same timetable. This is how the process begins. Individually
and corporately, life takes on new meaning. The tragedy happens when the questions come from self-appointed watchdogs
determined to keep us safe. They are absent of hunger and
its companion trait of humility. Revivals never start with the
watchdogs. *Never.*

The concern of something not being biblical takes center stage
as we try to eat the meat and throw away the bones. We all tend

to interpret what is before us by our knowledge of Scripture learned from our own history. The problem is that we all have limited knowledge and exposure to truth. Let's hope what we know is true, but what we know is also limited. That is true for all of us. Thus, what is happening can be completely from God, yet it will be rejected by some because it is different from what they have already experienced. It is quite humorous that most of them want God to do a new thing, as long as He does it the way He has always done it.

Some go into fear mode, thinking that emotional experiences are in excess, and that excess is our greatest danger. It is true that emotionalism has caused problems for the Church throughout history. But extreme emotionalism is easy to spot. Rather, the quiet unbelief and resistance from the skeptic is a far greater enemy. It is a powerful deceiver because it has become accepted in much of the world's church culture as wisdom and spiritual intelligence. It is neither. If we value something wrong, it has permission to stay.

Which is more dangerous, to interpret Scripture out of our experience, or to interpret it in the absence of experience? We would never embrace a teaching on prayer from one who has never prayed. I point that out not to say that any experience a person claims to have from God is really God. Nor should we redefine the meaning of the Bible because an angel showed up and spoke to someone differently from what is thought to be true. The Bible provides the absolute standard for life and ministry. But the fact remains that we interpret Scripture either out of experience or in its absence.

I know that approaching a move of God in this fashion is scary to some, perhaps to many. But when I look at the life of Christ and the relationship He had with the Father, and the demonstration of purity and power of the Holy Spirit that flowed from Him, I become jealous—jealous for what was made available to me by His example and commission. It seems illegal to desire anything less. Excess has been feared as long as I have been alive. I have chosen to turn the tables and fearfully concern myself with lack.

When I am in pursuit of rare expressions of the Gospel of the Kingdom found in the Person of Jesus Christ, I do so with people of like mind, staying accountable and humble, but at the same time, staying willing to risk all to obtain the lifestyle made available to all who embraced His "co-mission." The heartbeat of hope overrides all fears, enabling us to lean into what God is saying and doing. Living from this assurance brings such rest.

Prayer

Father, please give me true discernment in this hour for the challenges I face in order to step into a fuller expression of the Gospel as found in my Lord Jesus Christ. I long to see all that You have purposed for me in this life in both realms of purity and power. This is my hope. Please surround me with people of like heart and mind that I might illustrate this life in community. I pray these things that the name of Jesus would be exalted in all the earth.

Confession

God has purposed to do more in and through me than I could possibly imagine. I set my heart, therefore, to expect and anticipate the extraordinary life of Jesus to flow flawlessly through me. I was born for this purpose for His glory.

15

Love

Jesus messed up every funeral He
attended, including His own.

There are probably very few believers who do not get ex-
cited about what Jesus did as recorded in the gospels.
The gospels contain the living testimonies of the nature and
heart of God who loves people beyond our wildest dreams.
The challenge comes in our response to what He did, which
in some ways is determined by our response to a few pertinent
questions. Did the time of miracles end when the last apostle
died? Or did it end when the canon of Scripture was completed?
The idea of cessation is not in any way based on the revelation
of Scripture, itself. And it certainly cannot be found in the life,
teaching or prophecies of Jesus, who is perfect theology.

While some hold that view, their numbers are decreasing
continuously as the miracle ministry of Jesus is becoming more
and more evident in today's Church around the world. This is
especially true where the number of believers is increasing daily,
as recorded in Acts. The cessation of miracles is a doctrine
devised by the mind of man, created to comply with the belief
that the season for them no longer exists.

If, then, we do believe that miracles are for today, we face another question: Are they to happen solely as sovereign acts of God (where He initiates and we observe), or do we play a role in the outcome? Many of the former group are moving to the group that says miracles are possible, but only if God initiates. I am grateful for the forward motion, but that approach seems to nullify the fact that the disciples were commanded to heal the sick, raise the dead, etc. (see Matthew 10:8). They were not commanded to observe the sovereign invasions of God into impossible situations. That is a given, and is the joy of every believer. But there remains a command that requires obedience and pursuit on our part. Whether regarding a miracle of healing or the salvation of a soul, God often responds to our obedience.

The one other question that is worth considering here is this: If Jesus meant for us to be involved in healing the sick, raising the dead, etc., what standard do we follow? Did Jesus show us what God could do? Or was He showing us what a person could do who was in right relationship with God? I believe the latter. While Jesus was, and always has been, entirely God, He chose to live with the limitations of a man.

That brings us to this point: Did Jesus actually give us an example that could be followed by the average believer? I believe the answer is unquestionably yes!

Jesus Christ is perfect theology. He is love. And love changes things. There is no record of His attending a funeral and leaving the person dead. I do not think that means people are not to die, as Scripture says death is an appointment for every person. But Jesus seemed to run into situations where people died outside of God's timing. At minimum, we should at least attempt to do what Jesus did—including raise the dead.

The fear of looking foolish to others has kept many from responding to this command of the Lord. In addition, we might never do this assignment well. But that does not give me the right to change the assignment to what I do well, and then call that my ministry.

Prayer

Father, please help me not to get trapped in a life of human possibility. I want so much to represent You as Jesus did, illustrating the resurrection life Jesus made available to me. I want to think differently about situations that look hopeless and dead, realizing that nothing is impossible for You. Only when You say it is done do I want to back off my pursuit of breakthrough. Please help me with this.

Confession

I have purposed to spend the rest of my life learning what it means to live a life of resurrection power and presence. I know that it is in this way that I can best represent the Father of life as Jesus did. The example that Jesus gave me, along with His great commission, is enough for me to respond with a resounding yes! I will follow with all of my heart, to the glory of God our Father.

16

Faith

Faith grows through use.

Spending so much of my life in airplanes and sitting in meet-
ings is a prescription for health problems. Both exercise and
a healthy diet are vital to a successful lifestyle, let alone the vi-
brant one I want. I owe it to God to be at my best. I found that
these two areas are essential for the body as well as the soul. It
did not take long to realize that I am much more mentally alert
and creative when I am consistent in the discipline of exercise.
There is much to be said about the effect of being active and
eating well on the emotional life, too.

A number of years ago, I started lifting weights, as I could no
longer be active in the competitive sports of my youth. In doing
so, I found that I absolutely loved it! We picked up this activity as
a family and noticed very quickly its impact on our whole lives.
Not only were we sharper mentally, we actually started thinking
differently. For the first time in my life, I started looking at food
as fuel. It was not that taste did not matter, as God created food
for our pleasure. Rather it was the fact that I could tell the effect
of an early afternoon meal on the workout that evening. I do
not like doing things halfway, so I started studying the effects of
certain foods on the body as well as their effects on my strength
and energy levels. As a result, I began to eat for the workout.

This analogy works powerfully in the subject of faith. Faith is to our hearts/inner man what muscles are to our bodies. It is faith that enables the work of God to be done through us effectively. "Faith without works is dead" (James 2:26). We do not work to get faith. That kind of striving is anti-productive. But we do work to grow it, as faith grows with use. Everyone has been given a measure of faith. What we do with what we have determines how well we do in maturing as disciples of Jesus.

One additional insight on faith as learned from the world of exercise and fitness is the fact that sometimes we reach plateaus in our development. When a muscle reaches a plateau in its development, it needs to be shocked into growth. That can be done a number of different ways. One involves working the same muscle with a different exercise, hitting it from a different angle. Sometimes our faith becomes stagnant because we get stuck in a routine. In our walks with Christ we get accustomed to doing things a certain way. Yesterday's exercise that shocked our systems into great growth has become today's routine. In all the miracles of Jesus recorded in Scriptures, not one of them was done the same way as the previous one.

Prayer

Father, I believe You. I trust You. While I love the lessons of yesterday, I do not want them to confine me to a routine or formula. That is why I ask You to give me grace to hear Your voice always. It is my life. I always want to know what You are saying and what You are doing so I do not become stagnant in my faith. Thank You in advance for this answer to prayer.

Confession

I am a person of faith. I was born to believe God. Because of this, there is no need for me ever to become stagnant in my faith. I have set my heart to glorify Him by depending on His voice for my life.

17

Hope

Sometimes instead of answering our prayer, God gives us a promise.

We often treat prayer as though we are using a vending machine: We put in our requests, and, if we are lucky, we get the answers we want. We pray and God responds. While there is truth in that idea, it does not give the whole picture. Not by any means. Prayer is an expression of a relationship. It is the interaction of the Creator with His creation, bringing us into our eternal purpose. It is the school of God, training His people to rule and reign with Christ. Just knowing this simple principle gives hope for our entire walk with the Lord.

It is in God's nature to answer prayer. He loves satisfying the cries of our hearts. He is a father—the ultimate Father. Prayer represents the partnership between Him and those made in His likeness. But His heart's desire for us is much greater than answering our requests to be able to pay the electric bill or whatever it is that we are praying for. His desire to build people into His likeness through the proper use of His authority and power takes center stage as everything God does is unto this end—people who represent Him well, accurately.

A huge part of God's intention for us is to get us to live responsibly. That, of course, includes living righteously and not unto ourselves. But it is more. Living responsibly is to live with divine responsibility. It is to do as Jesus would do if He were in our shoes. But even that needs clarification because it is what Jesus—as the resurrected, ascended and glorified One—would do if He were in our shoes. The life of the believer is to illustrate the power and purpose of the resurrection over every enemy of humanity.

Our roles differ in the various seasons of our lives. In one moment, our job might be simply to stand by and see what God accomplishes for us. But then that changes, and we must become aware of the change. Instead of watching Him work, we work. But our work is not independent of Him. Quite the opposite. He works through us.

He arms us with purpose by giving us a promise instead of the answer. That way, we are forced to learn how to believe Him before the answer comes and then learn how to exercise His will in the circumstances that are contrary to the given promise. This is part of what it means to be a co-laborer with Christ. He labors, and we labor with Him.

Jesus was constantly training His disciples unto this end. That is why He taught them to speak to a mountain for it to be removed. It was His purpose behind cursing the fig tree that bore no fruit out of season. He led them into storms to see if they picked up the powerful lessons regarding their speech. It was in these lessons—outnumbering even His lessons on prayer—that His disciples were trained to implement and enforce the will of God on the earth. This is the assignment of every believer.

The answers to prayer reveal His goodness. When He gives us a promise instead of an answer, it reveals His desire to draw us into our eternal purpose. It is His longing to raise up people into their God-given responsibilities.

Prayer

Father, I need Your wisdom to know the differences between the seasons of my life. I want to know when to stand and watch You work on my behalf and when to embrace my responsibility to enforce Your purposes on the earth. Please give me clarity of heart and mind unto this end, that I might always live with rock-solid hope.

Confession

I have been given the privilege to pray and see God move on my behalf. And I have been given the great honor to take His promise and co-labor with Him to see His will accomplished on the earth. I embrace this assignment with fearful excitement, all for His glory.

18

Love

In grace, the ability to obey
comes in the command. In law,
you are left to perform.

One of the greatest bits of good news we could ever hear is that we are free from the Law. It is probably an over-simplification, but it basically means we no longer have to try to earn our righteousness through things we do or do not do, which, by the way, is impossible. For that reason we need a savior. The Law makes demands on behavior that no one has ever been able to keep—except for Jesus, that is, who actually fulfilled the requirements of the Law on our behalf, and once and for all satisfied its appetite.

One of the largest mistakes made in the discussion of law vs. grace is the notion that grace makes no demands on the believer—that law requires action and grace wants us just to "be." This simply is not true. While "abiding in Christ" is an amazing position of *rest* for the disciple who loves Jesus, it does not remove us from the need for action and obedience. The Law, for example, forbids murder. But the teaching of Jesus, the basis for the message of grace, says that it is just as wrong to be angry with a brother and call him names.

Wow! Let's be honest. It is much easier not to murder than it is not to get mad and call people names. Yet God sees the hostility of a name-caller as the seed of murder itself. If it grows and develops in an atmosphere of dishonor and rejection toward another until it is fully formed, it will conclude with murder. While it seldom does, from God's perspective the seed is as defiling as the fruit. And it is grace that gives the warning.

So how is it that grace can be more demanding than law? The profound nature of grace is not that it makes no requirements of us; it is that every command comes with the ability to perform it. Another way to state this, and perhaps a simpler one at that, is, *Law requires, grace enables.* That is the stunning difference between the two. When God speaks, He empowers. It is one of the most glorious examples of the Father's heart. His delight in us inspired the concept of co-laboring with us.

This beautiful partnership between the Infinite One and His finite creation is illustrated well in Ezekiel 2:1–2: "Then He said to me, 'Son of man, stand on your feet that I may speak with you!' As He spoke to me the Spirit entered me and set me on my feet; and I heard Him speaking to me." God told Ezekiel to stand up. The next thing he knew the Holy Spirit stood him up. The message is not that God does things for us that we are capable of doing ourselves. Previous to this work of the Spirit in him, the prophet Ezekiel was lying prostrate before the Lord of glory, incapable of moving. So the Lord gave him a command and then enabled him to do it. The same concept is repeated over and over again through this Gospel of the Kingdom. He commands us to heal the sick, when we have no ability to do so. Yielding to the command to do the impossible is what connects us to the enabling grace of God. Abiding in His love enables us to love.

James highlights this concept with this statement: "In humility receive the word implanted, which is able to save your souls" (James 1:21). Where is salvation's ability? It is in the Word. This is the best picture of the process of grace. Humility is the condition of the tender heart. It receives seed, the Word of God. It is the word of grace that brings the capacity to perform what is commanded.

Prayer

Heavenly Father, I love Your voice and am alive because You speak to me. Thank You so much for Your generous word of promise and hope. Help me to recognize the times You have spoken to me things that I know I cannot do but am being "graced" to do. I do not want my small thinking to cripple my potential when You see things differently from me. I receive your Word with humility, confessing that all breakthroughs are for Your glory!

Confession

I confess with Mary, when she faced the most impossible assignment ever, "Be it unto me according to Your word." The impossible is now possible, because my Father commands me to do it. I embrace His Word with a humble heart that I might present to Him the fruit of the impossible. And I abide in His love for me, which in turn enables me to love, for the glory of God.

19

Faith

The way you think either expresses faith or undermines faith.

F aith affects our thoughts. Our thoughts also affect our faith. Winning the battle over the mind is central to developing the Christlike lifestyle. It would be a grave mistake, however, to think that faith comes from the mind. It does not. It comes from the heart.

Faith is not intellectual in nature. The Scriptures say, "By faith we understand. . . ." It is not the other way around. Faith helps the mind grasp things that would normally be out of reach and sets the mind up for development in a healthy way. True faith is superior to reason. Yet the renewed mind is also important—it enhances the life of faith in the way that banks of a river affect the water rushing past. It provides a course defined by divine purpose.

Faith affects my thoughts because my thinking is consistent with and shaped by God's promises over my life. In that case, fear no longer defines me, as I live with the conviction that God has an answer for every situation. But it does not stop with the conviction that there are answers to difficult or impossible situations. I must also think differently about myself and others, according to His heart. Faith corrects perceptions and aligns us with the heart of God for others. This allows us to do as Jesus did when He called the zealous, but unstable, Peter a rock. Jesus saw correctly. Others did not.

A renewed mind sees from divine perspective. In our lives, it is the result of repentance, as repentance basically means to change the way we think. It considers realms of possibility that are not natural, or perhaps more accurately are *beyond nature*. Those without Christ at the center of their thinking live within a prison of restraints that God never intended. Fear often dictates how people think, but fear never bears the fruit of the impossible. Wisdom should address more than survival; wisdom should lead to Kingdom-orientated breakthroughs.

How would your thinking change if nothing were impossible, if there were no regrets haunting you from your past, if you had unlimited resources to accomplish all your purpose on the earth? Faith affects human reasoning by removing the boundaries and obstacles we have become accustomed to. It is time to let faith have its full effect on our minds. Let's just see what might be possible in our lifetimes.

Prayer

Father, I never want my repentance to be on the surface only. I want to be moved deeply unto repentance, as I must think Your thoughts and see from Your perspective. May all the attitudes and thoughts of my heart please You at all times. I want the mind of Christ to become my daily possession—my daily expression. Be glorified in how I think.

Confession

The mind of Christ is my inheritance. I will not strive for what has been given to me freely. By grace I will think in a way that both glorifies God and establishes me in a faith that changes things.

20

Hope

Thankfulness and hunger create
the atmosphere for increase.

To come into the answers that we hope for, we must steward well the moments that we have in God. I do not believe we earn answers, but I do believe we can hinder them from coming by not responding to the ways of His Kingdom. To steward these moments well, we must pay attention to what God values. While the list is long, the two most necessary traits are thankfulness and hunger. Those two aspects of hope, held in tension, help us to press onward, but they also help us maintain a proper heart toward Him "until the answer comes." This abiding hope is our assurance . . . until.

We pray out of hunger. Desire takes on supernatural characteristics as it drives us into the presence of the Lord to bring a request. But sometimes the Lord answers a prayer differently than we expected. I have seen Him answer prayer in seed form instead of the full breakthrough we were looking for. Thankfulness is critical at that point.

One of my favorite stories in the Bible is when Jesus multiplied the food. John 6:11 says that they were able to feed the multitudes with the small portion of food *after He had given thanks* for what He had. That is a pretty remarkable statement. The little was made large in the atmosphere of thanksgiving.

I have watched so many times through the years as people abort their own miracles. Let me give you an example. Let's say a person has no movement in her left arm because of a frozen shoulder, and she comes for prayer. As I pray, she begins to move her arm, but not yet with full movement. So she can now move it about eighteen inches from her side, but then it is as though she hits a wall. Almost every time that person will say, "No, it's not healed yet."

One thing I hate is hype. I never want anyone to pretend a miracle has happened when it has not. But what actually happened in this case? In one moment, she had no movement. In the next, she has eighteen inches of movement. It is obviously not where we want it to be, but why is thankfulness so rare at this point? If I were saving my money with a goal of having $10,000 to buy something very important for my family, and someone gave me a check for $3,000, would I be thankful? Of course I would! I am heading in the right direction. So it is with healing or other kinds of miracles. Sometimes the Lord gives us a seed. And it is the atmosphere of thanksgiving that releases that seed into its potential.

The food multiplied for Jesus after He gave thanks. When He was thankful for a boy's lunch, it became enough to feed thousands. Thankfulness has that kind of power, both over us and over our circumstances.

If there were one characteristic that I could *wish* upon the people of God, it would be thankfulness. There is nothing so life-transforming in its impact on attitude and conduct as that simple trait. And it is that trait that releases the supernatural potential of God's promises over all that concerns us.

Prayer

Father, I need to see things as You do. Then I know I would be thankful all the time. You have been so good to me, and You deserve the honoring response of thankfulness from me in all situations. Help me to take advantage of the opportunities that lie before me that seem so intimidating and invade them with a thankful heart. And please help me not just to use this as a tool for breakthrough, but, instead, let it be the honest expression of my hopeful heart for Your faithfulness to me. Thank You.

Confession

God is good and God is faithful; this is my reason for hope. He has given Himself to the things that concern me. Because of this, I will honor Him with thanksgiving before the answer comes. I will honor Him while the answer is developing before my eyes. And once the breakthrough is in full form, I will continue to declare His greatness. For He is worthy of all honor.

21

Love

Bible study without Bible experience is pointless.

It is not possible to overemphasize the value of the Word of God for our lives. It is our life, our food, our daily bread. And while it is not possible to overemphasize, it is possible to distort. The religious leaders of Jesus' day did that very well. Jesus confronted one of those distortions when He said, "You search the Scriptures because you think that in them you have eternal life; it is these that testify about Me; and you are unwilling to come to Me so that you may have life" (John 5:39–40). Life is the goal of reading the Bible. Life is measured in its freedoms, its newness. The transformation of a person is the end product of the study of Scriptures. We live by every word that comes from His mouth.

Tragically, people who have no encounter with the One the Scriptures point to are often the most critical judges of others. They end up working against the very thing they think they are working for.

Granted, as I mentioned earlier, great error has come into the Church when experience is valued over Scripture. Legitimate horror stories exist in which great deception entered a person's life or even a group of people, a movement, when they interpreted the Bible through their experiences. Generally, in these cases, the people came up with their own interpretations of Scripture that, in their minds, were new and fresh. Or perhaps they saw an angel or had a vision or something unusual happened that led them off the cliff of reasoning. The end for these individuals is deception and bondage.

I have seen this firsthand, actually. And it should be a concern for anyone who is hungry for what the Bible speaks of. But it is no less dangerous to interpret Scripture apart from experience. Again, would you receive the insights and instruction on what it means to be born again from someone who was not? I doubt it.

Many people criticize those who long to experience more in God, but I don't trust the ones who don't. We are not going to be kept free from deception by abandoning experience. In fact, the ones who do not hunger more for God are already deceived.

Oftentimes religious circles are known for extreme control of the people, situations and environment around them. Control then becomes the issue of the hour. Studying the Scriptures without letting the Holy Spirit teach us puts us in control. He always takes us to Jesus. Going to the One the Scriptures point to puts Him in control. In other words, when the Bible is an end unto itself, it gives us a measure of learning, but no personal transformation.

One of the primary issues that Jesus had with the scribes and Pharisees was their approach to the Scriptures. They were very learned by the educational standards around them. They could quote, recite and teach others the commands of God, along with the commands they created from what they thought God wanted. But they could not do what they taught others to do. There was no impartation of grace that actually enabled them to obey the Word they studied.

The bottom line was that they had no relationship with the Person they studied about; therefore, there was no enablement to obey. They missed the most important part of the life they thought they had said yes to—to live in, enjoy and give away God's love. They were not even close.

I love God's Word so much. It is alive. It speaks. The more I read, the more I want to read. Hunger for wisdom and understanding has to be the most natural hunger there is for the disciple of Jesus. Reading the Bible with my heart wide open moves me to greater surrender in pursuit of the One all the Scriptures point to—Jesus. It is good for me to remember that if for some reason hunger wanes, there is a practical solution. In this Kingdom, you get hungry by eating.

Prayer

Father, I love the gift of hunger You have given me. I trust You never to give me a stone instead of bread. All my trust is in You. You are the perfect Father, the God of perfect love, delighting in us beyond our ability to delight in ourselves. Thank You for that. And as I daily read Your Word, please help me to see what I need to see and be changed into everything You planned for my life from the beginning.

Confession

I love the Bible. I love that God makes it the living testimony of my wonderful Savior, Jesus Christ. I embrace the privilege of encountering the One the Scriptures point to. I delight in all it says about me and purpose to change my thoughts accordingly. By God's grace, I will succeed in these things that God may be glorified!

22

Faith

We are designed to invade the impossible.

It is a wonderful thing to see God use natural talents and resources to accomplish His purposes. Surrendering these areas of our lives to His use is both vital and refreshing. But it is tragic when the high point of the believer's life is accomplishing something that is humanly possible. Building buildings, raising funds for projects, giving ourselves to meet basic needs of people all must be done! That is the practical side of our faith. But most accomplishments of this nature could also be done by any of the many human-interest clubs in our cities. All we need to reach those goals is people, talent and money. While these accomplishments are important, they must not be considered the ultimate examples of this life of faith. We must be known for practical service, *plus*. It is the *plus* that often gets forgotten. The *plus* is the impossible.

The Spirit of the resurrected Christ lives in every believer. Resurrection power from another world, which is far beyond reason, defines our nature as followers of Jesus. Invading the impossible is our birthright. It gives Him the chance to manifest His heart for people, going beyond what can be done in the natural. This is another situation of Kingdom living that is not either/ or. We must build the buildings, support missionaries, feed the poor and all the other things we do that effectively demonstrate the heart of God. But those things will never satisfy either the heart of the believer or the heart of the pre-believer longing for a relationship with almighty God. The liar, destroyer and thief must be stopped. For that to happen, we need more than money and time. We need power, the kind that Jesus carried into the darkness of His day.

Jesus illustrated these things a bit differently from the way the Church has learned to do them. He worked to destroy the works of the devil, which are death, loss and destruction. Wherever those three things exist, we see the devil's fingerprints. And those fingerprints reveal our assignment. By nature that means our job is to bring resurrection as an answer to death, gain as an answer to loss, and restoration as an answer to destruction. Jesus was extremely practical. But being practical for Him is different from being practical for us. Our idea of practical is training seeing-eye dogs to help the blind. Jesus' idea of practical was healing the blind. Practical in His world is impractical in ours, yet completely necessary. His assignment is our assignment.

Jesus' commission was to invade the impossible. Our time and talents are important, but they are not going to get the Great Commission done.

Prayer

Father, I really need Your help with this one. I often reduce Your will to what I can do with or without You. Forgive me for that. Help me to see the surrounding situations the same way Jesus would see them. I want to illustrate Your heart for people with my money and time, but also with what You have given me from Your world—the power of heaven. I will embrace Your heart until Your heart becomes mine.

Confession

I was designed for the impossible. It is my inheritance to see the impossibilities of life bend their knees to the name of Jesus through my lips. I will continue to give and serve, but I will also believe until the power of God is seen in me. I long for this that God may receive glory in all the earth!

23

Hope

It takes courage to expect the
best. Anyone without hope
can expect the worst.

Reading newspapers or watching the news on television
exposes us to levels of bad news in proportions unheard
of before this generation. This is the generation of instant
information. We can know in moments of a tragedy or crisis
from the other side of the planet. On top of that, bad news
sells.

Following the terrorist attacks on the United States in September 2001, most of us Americans were glued to our TV sets
many hours a day to catch the latest possible explanation of what
happened and why. I am not saying that was wrong. And I am
not saying that news agencies never report good news. But their
business cannot survive solely on positive reports. Many years
ago one of the Christian publishers in the United States tried
to create a newspaper with only good news. It went bankrupt.
Good news does not sell, even to believers.

My wife is the best at *praying through the news* of anyone
I know. She does so because she lives with an overriding hope,
no matter what. It is a viable way of staying informed, yet living

proactively by bringing about God's answers to a crazy, mixed-up world. Yet the problem remains—even for intercessors who pray over the news. If we are not careful, the steady stream of bad news will cloud our awareness of what God is saying and doing. Deception sets in that positions us to live and act defensively instead of continuing to respond to God's leading.

Such an inundation of bad reports can create a strange situation for the believer: We learn to become encouraged through bad news. Since we seemingly cannot solve the enormity of crisis around the world, the only thing left is to look at it as a sign of the times. We say something like, "Well, it's just another indication that we are in the last days." Being encouraged from bad news is a perversion. The enemy chooses this strategy of bombarding our minds, wanting to dull our hope for the future. Hopelessness attracts the demonic.

When Jesus declared that there would be "wars and rumors of wars," He was not giving us a promise; He was describing the conditions into which He was sending His last day's army. We are here to make a difference.

When we recognize a spiritual climate that is different from that of the King and His Kingdom, we have to live intentionally in the opposite spirit to that prevailing climate. If we fail to do this, we will be influenced by that negative atmosphere. We are designed by God to be a people of extraordinary hope.

Learning how to maintain hope is one of the most important parts of the believer's life—primarily because we attract what we are looking for. So look for good news. Look for reports of what God is doing in the world. The numbers of conversions in this hour are staggering. The sheer numbers of people being raised from the dead are beyond comprehension. Church planting is at an all-time high. The transformation of cities and nations is climbing rapidly. The leaders of nations and industries are turning to Jesus in record numbers. These things are true, absolutely true.

Examine Scripture for His promises for the last days. The Bible is filled with stunning promises for the time we live in. If they become part of your steady diet, you will never again be encouraged by bad news. Instead, you will be a fountain of hope to everyone around you. Hope is a magnet. You will attract into your life people who are looking for the answers you carry.

Prayer

Heavenly Father, thank You for making me a citizen of Your world, even though I am still alive on planet earth. Help me to live with the hope that is consistent with Your promises. I know that darkness has never intimidated You. I do not want ever again to fall for the lie that darkness is winning. I honor You for the fact that of the increase of Your government there will be no end! Your expression of rule is only increasing. Help me to see it and convey it well to the world around me.

Confession

I am an agent of hope—the undying, unending hope that my Father has given me. I will not react to the powers of darkness. Instead, I will respond to what God is saying and doing. This is my privileged position in life. And this I will do to the glory of God.

24

Love

One of the great tragedies in life
is for the Bible to be interpreted
by people who are not in love.

When my need to appear right is greater than my desire to display God's love, I will inevitably treat people with judgment, disrespect and harshness. The Old Testament is filled with so many disasters that it is not hard to pick up an angry approach to life and ministry. That is, until you consider Jesus.

This is why I stress the importance of letting the Holy Spirit be our teacher when we read the Bible. Otherwise, it is much too easy to get angry. The Holy Spirit helps us read the Scriptures with the provision that Jesus is the answer. Without Him, we just see the rules.

Have you ever considered that much of the Church today is known for what we oppose—rather than for love? Take politics. Much of the Church raises protest banners, writes letters of criticism and publicly denounces politicians and other public figures for their sinful ways. Various Christian organizations have orchestrated boycotts to force people in power to yield to scriptural principles. There is a place for that, and it works in measure. But it is often partnering with a political spirit to accomplish Kingdom purposes. The process will cost us eventually.

Jesus said, "If you live by the sword, you'll die by the sword" (see Matthew 26:52). The way we choose to live is the way we choose to die. Whatever is gained through, in this case, a political spirit has to be maintained by a political spirit, which uses the fear of man as a tool of manipulation to obtain a desired outcome. In other words, the end justifies the means. The spirit that promotes us will ultimately be the one that takes us down. But Jesus functioned differently, completely differently.

Sinners sought the chance to be with Jesus. The thieving tax collector, Zacchaeus, climbed a tree just to get a glimpse of Him. Upon noticing this man in a tree, Jesus invited Himself to Zacchaeus' house for a meal. The prostitute broke all protocol to enter a religious leader's home just to weep at Jesus' feet and wash them with her tears. The list of such encounters is impressive throughout the gospels. Any harshness from Jesus was always aimed at religious leaders who defiled His message by keeping people away from the freedom He provided.

People who are not in love see things differently. History is filled with crazy people who used the Bible to justify their hatred. They considered any opposition to be persecution, which only confirmed for them the correctness of their approach to life.

Jesus, on the other hand, suffered persecution because of His love. The freedom He offered upset the power struggle of religious leaders who kept the nation in fear. It is interesting that Jesus did not intimidate the sinners and lowly people around Him; nor did they withdraw from Him because of His purity. He lived in perfect holiness without compromise, yet attracted those considered to be the greatest sinners of His day. True holiness is the essence of real beauty.

Love changes everything. It changes how we read the Bible, and what we see when we read the Bible. Without love, we see hopelessness. We lose sight of the promises and respond with judgment. In the absence of love, we often move in anger, calling it righteous indignation. Yes, judgments are found in the Bible, but love looks for answers and solutions from our loving Father, who is more committed to our well-being than we are. Those who are not in love see only the requirements God has given and not His willingness to unleash heaven's power on earth, *gracing* us into victory. Such enablement is His gift to all who receive Him.

Prayer

Heavenly Father, thank You for giving us Your Word, the Holy Scriptures. You continually give me life from what I read. Thank You for that. Please help me to read everything through the life of Jesus, with the Holy Spirit as my guide. I never want my desire for correctness to be greater than my love for You and for people. In fact, let my passion for truth come only as an expression of my love for You. I know these things are possible only through Your grace. Thank You in advance for enabling me to put love first.

Confession

By the grace of God freely given to me, I will display my love for God and His Word by my practical love for people. Even in my pursuit of truth, I will illustrate the heart of Jesus for others by caring for those who differ from me. And all these things I will do that God may be glorified.

25

Faith

You have authority over any storm you can sleep in.

J esus set the standard for how we face life-threatening storms
effectively—in rest. The storm mentioned in Mark 4:36–41
brought great fear to the disciples. They probably thought they
were going to die. What made the moment even more confusing was that Jesus did not seem to care; instead, He chose to
sleep in the stern of the boat on a cushion. When they finally
woke Him, they asked Him why He did not care that they were
perishing. He got up and rebuked the wind, and released peace
over the sea. He then asked them why they had no faith. This
moment illustrates how the Kingdom works, how faith works:
It works from rest.

I have seen countless times when believers were tormented by
great fear in a horrible situation and rebuked the devil accordingly. It usually involved yelling, tears and threats. But I have
honestly never seen the devil yield to such tactics. Not that raising our voices is wrong. There is just a great difference between
the loud voice of faith and the loud voice of fear. And believe
me, the devil knows the difference. The voice of faith repels

him, while the voice of fear attracts him. The words spoken make little difference.

This place of rest can also be called abiding in Christ. Jesus taught of this in His story about the vine and the branches. In the same way that a branch is connected to the vine, so we are to be connected to Christ. Abiding in Christ must become practical again. *Abiding* means basically that we live with a profound connection to the heart, mind and presence of God, with His promises. Living conscious of God's heart for us keeps us in a place of peace. And peace is more than the absence of something like war, noise or conflict. Our peace is the presence of Someone. It is the actual atmosphere of heaven.

When we begin to live out of fear, we must return to wherever we left our peace. Losing our peace usually involves making a mental agreement with a lie until our emotions become captive to that lie. The fiery darts of the enemy get past our shields of faith and penetrate our souls. The agreements made in those moments work against God's purposes for our lives. Repentance is in order. Repentance is the deep sorrow for sin that provokes a change in thinking. It is not complete until our thought lives are affected. It is not complete until we see that His promises and purposes are within reach.

The easiest approach to this challenge in life is to maintain peace in the first place. Cultivate a supreme value for the presence of God upon your life. Always have God's promises for your life within reach. Memorize them, sing them, write them out on pieces of paper—do anything you need to do to keep His mind in front of yours, until His thoughts become instinctively your thoughts.

Prayer

Father, please give me some kind of warning when I am about to leave the place of peace You have created for me to live in. I do not

*want to do that anymore. It is too hard to recover. Remind me of
the truth when I am about to consider a lie. And help me to anchor
my soul in Your presence, in Your peace. Thank You for giving me
the actual atmosphere of heaven to dwell in now.*

Confession

*His peace is my portion. It is my possession forever. I choose to live
aware of the Holy Spirit upon me, and will not forget that His
thoughts about me are all good.*

26

Hope

You will always reflect the nature of the world you are most aware of.

This world is filled with mistrust, skepticism and unbelief. Faith exists, but rarely is it the cultural norm. As a result, most believers are more aware of the darkness around them than the heavenly realm of which they are citizens. This failure to recognize that our present-day citizenship is in heaven costs us tremendously. Not just when we die, but now, in this present darkness.

People release the reality of the world they are most aware of, good or bad. We know this instinctively. We know, for example, that if a depressed person walks into a room, no one will be healed by his shadow (see Acts 5:15–16). The picture is obvious. Depression often comes from believing a lie. Being absorbed with a lie affects a person's countenance, which has an impact on the atmosphere around him. It is not a countenance of life, encouragement and health. Such an individual often drains anything positive from the environment, as he looks for something to get him through the next hour.

Or take, for another example, people filled with bitterness. Rather than draining the atmosphere, they fill the air with tension and conflict. They contaminate the environment, releasing what they are most aware of—offense, conflict and division No one will be healed by their shadows either.

The great news is that light is greater than darkness. Anyone living aware of the presence of God is never at the mercy of those who darken the environment, whether those people are bitter or depressed or whatever. And it goes even further. As we live aware of the presence of God with us, we are much more likely to influence the environment ourselves. It is true.

The Old Testament gives us a profound illustration of this principle in the life of Lot. Second Peter 2:7 tells us that God "rescued righteous Lot, oppressed by the sensual conduct of unprincipled men." While Lot did not have the same benefits that we have in the New Covenant—that is, the indwelling presence of the Holy Spirit—others in the Old Covenant seemed to have more success with that challenge than did Lot. Daniel is a perfect case in point. He lived in a demonic society, was numbered with the witches and warlocks of his day and worked for a demented king named Nebuchadnezzar who demanded worship from his subjects. But Daniel did not buckle under the influence of the surrounding darkness. His ability to live above it all no doubt played a part in his significant role in one of the greatest conversions in all of Scripture—that of Nebuchadnezzar himself.

Lot's surroundings were more than he could bear. And even though he was righteous, he became oppressed by the evil in others. It literally shut down the influence that God intended for him to have. We can be thankful that that result is not inevitable for believers, because, where sin abounds, we carry the promise that grace abounds more. Grace flows through believing believers. We can affect our surroundings by our partnership with the Presence of God—by carrying His promises in our hearts. We can manifest the King's dominion in the environment around us. People possessed with hope are able to endure, and endure well. Hope attracts breakthrough.

Prayer

Father, please help me to live aware of You in the same way Jesus was. He was continually aware of what You were doing and saying, and I want the same thing. Thank You that Jesus made it possible for me to live in the same measure of victory that He did. I give You praise and honor for the fact that You designed me as a carrier of Your presence and have given me the privilege of bringing Your presence to a lost and dying world.

Confession

God has enabled me to live above the influence of evil around me. I celebrate the fact that, according to 1 John 4:4, greater is He who is in me than he who is in the world. And that greatness will be seen through me as I live in the constant adoration of God through the Holy Spirit.

27

Love

Sympathy is the counterfeit of compassion.

Much of what has been applauded as Christlike compassion is nothing more than sympathy. Sympathy has little to no hope and lives without power. It leaves a person with his affliction, problem or question, while compassion brings him out. Jesus, again, set the standard on this subject. Whenever He was "moved with compassion," a miracle followed—every single time. His view of compassion is much different from ours, so ours must change. It is as though compassion was the vehicle that God's power rode upon. All ministry is supposed to be that way—gifts riding upon the vehicle of character. Gifts and character were never meant to be separated.

Sympathy can even become dangerous, as it reinforces a person's identity in his affliction or need. The best that the natural man can come up with, sympathy tends to insulate the person in need from awareness of God's promises that are for now, therefore keeping him from the faith necessary to overcome.

The religious spirit loves for us to operate in sympathy as it celebrates *form without power*. It fuels people's identity as victims and makes the possibility of heaven in the future their only hope. While that may sound okay, it is not how Jesus lived or what He preached. His message was that *the Kingdom of God is at hand*, here and now and within reach. While the eternal aspect will be glorious beyond measure, it is the *now* that was the target of His message, backed by His works, that destroyed the devil's works.

Let's be honest: It is often much easier to console and give sympathy, knowing there is no simple answer for a person's problem. Tragically, we position ourselves to comfort instead of contend for the miracle on behalf of those who cannot seem to fight for themselves. It is easier than putting our faith on the line.

Biblical compassion is the love of God. Love seeks the best. And the believing believer has access to the best—Kingdom power being released now. Faith operates through love. These two things are eternally connected.

Compassion has Kingdom solutions in sight. It is energized by the affection of God, the One who paid a high price for us to be healed and delivered in this life. He does not look at a problem wondering if He should provide an answer. He does not look at a disease and wonder whether or not to give healing. Two thousand years ago, a price was paid for all to be healed. In the same way that payment made it possible for all of us to be forgiven. There is no lack on His end of the equation.

Prayer

My Father and my God, I need grace in a very big way each and every day. Help me not to insulate people from their need to trust You. Instead, I want Your affection to flow through me, not only giving comfort to those in need, but also bringing them into breakthroughs. Help me to recognize Your heart for each person and demonstrate Your kindness in the same way Jesus would. People must know what You are like, and I give my life unto this end, that You might be glorified.

Confession

I will not restrict my life to what is humanly possible. Instead, I will embrace the privilege of allowing His heart of love and compassion to flow through me. As I demonstrate His perfect compassion, I will look for and anticipate the answers that Jesus would bring were He in my place. These are the things I will do that Jesus Christ will be exalted in all the earth.

28

Faith

A stronghold is anything people trust other than God.

Trust is the expression of faith. And whenever people put their trust in something other than God, the enemy of our souls sees it as a place of legal access to deepen the deception. His goal is to inhabit it and make it a stronghold. The powers of darkness are attracted to misplaced trust. They do not really care where trust is placed, as long as it is not in God. That is why Paul said, "Don't give place to the devil." It is possible for a believer to give the devil the place reserved for God alone.

The book of Proverbs gives us an interesting picture that illustrates this truth: "A wise man scales the city of the mighty and brings down the stronghold in which they trust" (Proverbs 21:22). The key phrase is *stronghold in which they trust*. If you can see where people have put their trust other than God, you will find the stronghold that must be brought down. Wisdom enables us to bring down the strongholds over cities once they have been removed from our own lives.

Jesus modeled a strict lifestyle for those wanting to be His disciples. Their approach to family, money, relationships, occupations and the like was different from the approach of the world around them. Some think mistakenly that Jesus taught poverty as a lifestyle. That simply is not true. The disciples had to go without in order to learn how to steward correctly what God would provide for them. Their journey was much like the children of Israel's journey in the wilderness. They went without in order to learn how to manage the land of promises they were about to inherit. Before Jesus left the earth, He urged them to take the money belts with them that they were forbidden to take at the beginning. It was never about money; it was about trust.

The challenge for us is not whether or not we should have money; the challenge is where we are going to put our trust in spite of how little or how much we have. How much is too much money? Whatever amount replaces trust. For one person, it is little. For another, it is a lot.

Anything that earns our trust, besides God, attracts the demonic. The devil considers all misplaced trust as devil worship, for he hides himself in its shadows.

Faith also attracts. But instead of empowering darkness, we become like lightning rods that attract the activities of God into our surroundings. Even the angels are compelled to fill such an atmosphere, for they have been assigned to "render service for the sake of those who will inherit salvation" (Hebrews 1:14). They are fascinated with our trust in our Redeemer because it is a position they will never have.

Trusting in God is a privilege. It is worth every effort we make to expose ourselves to and memorize the promises of God for our lives. I had a dear friend named Dick Mills, who is now home with the Lord. He memorized 7,700 promises in the Bible, in various translations. He was a joy to be around, for he always had a promise from God for any problem or challenge. He brought encouragement to countless thousands of people through his years of faithful service to the Lord.

This should be the normal lifestyle for the believer. For this is really the lifestyle of one abiding in Christ—always mindful of His presence and His Word, burning with God's promise for every situation. This is the atmosphere of heaven that is becoming the atmosphere on earth.

Prayer

Father, please help me never to give place to the devil by trusting in anything that is in conflict with Your heart for me. I know You are fully trustworthy. Help me to see the promises that You placed in Your Word just for me. I do not want to think according to my limitations, but according to Your promises. Let me be one who is possessed by Your promises, bringing hope to everyone around me, regardless of the circumstances.

Confession

I choose to meditate on God's promises for me. I cannot afford to have a thought in my mind that is not in His. So today I declare that my trust is in God alone, as He has already prepared everything necessary for me to be successful in this challenge.

29

Hope

I try to live in such a way that
nothing becomes bigger than
my awareness of God.

Most of us know what it is to be so bothered by something that we worry for hours or days, sometimes to the point of being unable to sleep at night. Try as we might to change the subject in our heads, we are unable to let go. In part, it is the result of the effort of the enemy to distract us from the promises of God for our lives. He is hoping we will lose track of the tools that God has given us for imminent victory.

As negative as it is to be so absorbed with a problem that we cannot sleep, it is encouraging in this sense: It reveals that we actually know how to meditate. We just need to change the subject matter.

In cultic meditation, people empty their minds. That is dangerous because many spirits are looking for entrance into a person's life to bring the influence of darkness. Empty minds are invitations to the demonic. Biblical meditation is quite different. It means to fill our minds with what God says, running it over and over in our minds and hearts until the truth takes root in us. What God says then becomes more than something we quote; it becomes a part of who we are.

Whatever we think about or focus on affects our attitudes and countenances immensely. And while faith does not come from the mind, our thoughts and attitudes have great effect on our faith. Simply put, the devil wants us to be overwhelmed by his work on the earth. He knows that if he can undermine our hope, he has influence over what and how we think, and ultimately weaken our faith.

The devil comes to kill, steal and destroy. In present-day culture, we are fed a constant diet of news about death, loss and destruction—the devil's fingerprints. And if I dwell on what he has done, I will live in reaction to him—and he is not worthy of affecting my agenda. He simply is not worthy of having any influence on my thoughts, plans or actions.

We all face challenges. Sometimes the problems are very personal and heart-wrenching. Sometimes they affect the lives of people close to us. Sometimes they have to do with a crisis, such as a life-threatening storm or war or threats of international conflict. I have no recourse in problems if they overwhelm me. I must be convinced of God's overriding goodness, as well as the abiding presence of the Holy Spirit in my life. When I stay conscious of Him, I can become part of the answer. If I become overly concerned with the problem, though, I am more likely to become a complainer who spiritualizes such weakness by calling it intercession.

Please note that I emphasize living aware of the Holy Spirit in and upon me more than the problem. In other words, I am not just looking for a doctrinal statement to make me feel better in the situation. I am looking for Him, the Person of the Holy Spirit. I am looking to recognize the One in whom is all safety, victory and joy, who continually positions me for triumph to the glory of Jesus' name.

It sounds rather simple really: Stay more aware of God than of problems. At least for me, the practice of such a priority is more challenging than the concept. Yet the truth remains. Whatever I focus on will determine if I am a victor in or a victim of the problems around me.

Prayer

Father God, please help me to stay aware of the wonderful gift of the Holy Spirit. Thank You for giving Yourself to me so completely! I do not want to become a victim. I want to live in such a way that Your purposes and plans for the world around me come into fruition. Thank You for letting me be a part of the company of people who live to change the world. May You receive all the glory for every area of breakthrough in and through my life.

Confession

I am uniquely designed to carry the presence of God in a way that helps others to become victorious, giving Him all the glory. I embrace this privileged assignment for the glory of God.

30

Love

Honor is the atmosphere in which the
people of God become their best.

Increasing emphasis has been given in recent years to the subject of honor. In our family and church, we have worked to develop what we call "the culture of honor." It is more than an action; it is a core value that affects all of life. And as such, its importance is hard to exaggerate.

Honor comes from a heart of excellence. Honor is how we display value. If I had a priceless vase, I probably would not put it on the back patio where it would be exposed to the weather or my young grandchildren. I would create a safe place for it where I could display its beauty for anyone who enters my home. It would have a place of honor.

Honor is one of the clearest expressions of love that I know. It creates a healthful and purposeful environment that enables people to become their best. Consider this: There is an act of honor, and then there is a lifestyle of honor. The latter acts like a greenhouse. It is an environment that enables the plants—the family, workplace or church—to grow more easily. An honorable lifestyle creates the atmosphere that enables the growth of all things good.

Leaders who want a culture of honor so they will be treated better miss the point entirely. That would be like a father or mother coming home from work expecting the whole family to rally around him or her, tending to every need. I used to remind myself on my way home from a day at the office, "Bill, you're not off work yet. You still have four hours." In other words, my wife had worked hard all day caring for the children. She needed my love, my help and support. My kids had been without their dad all day, and they wanted and needed to play. As I walked through the door, I could hear the sound of tiny feet running toward me and voices yelling, "Daddy!" It was the most beautiful sound in the whole world. To ignore that and then require them to serve me would have been absolutely heartless and foolish. I hugged and kissed my wife and then wrestled with my kids. Giving them time and pleasure was giving them honor. By honoring them, I got better, too. The difficult issues of the day seemed to disappear in the atmosphere created for the sake of others.

As a leader, I am the one who sets the standard for how honor will be lived out. If my culture of honor is based on corporate structure, it will do nothing more than exalt the greatest at the expense of the least. That is how the *corporate ladder* was formed. Many churches function this way. Honor has become the act of giving to those who are powerful, with special attention for those who have achieved much. Rather, honor should be given before there is the capacity to achieve. It should be given based on who people are, not just what they have done. The infant on my lap and the toddler in my arms are incapable of achieving much. But loving them and giving them honor happens because I see what is yet unseen. The heart that honors others sees things in them that they do not see. It is as though God opens the eyes of the honorable because He can trust them to give the response of love.

A true culture of honor must have impact on the least among us, or it is not really our culture. And because that atmosphere draws out the potential of people long before they see it in themselves, it has that greenhouse effect. Honor brings out the greatness that lies hidden.

In our homes, places of employment and churches, we "do life" with other believers. Our relationships within these areas are healthier if we approach them with the concept of healthy family life. Once we leave the concept of family, we leave the concept of Kingdom. It is this approach that makes living with honor—the true expression of love—possible.

Prayer

Heavenly Father, You honor me as Your child, even though I do not fully understand all that is meant by that expression of Your great love. By Your grace operating in me, I purpose to honor others into their potential. Please help me to see the moments that I might miss and display Your love in a way that honors people and glorifies You. This is the culture I embrace for the glory of God!

Confession

God Himself has honored me by calling me His own. I did nothing to earn this honor, yet He gives it to me liberally. I declare that it is my privilege to recognize the significance of others and display it through honor. For I know that when I have done this for the least among us, I have done it for God Himself.

31

Ignorance asks for understanding;
unbelief asks for proof.

Zacharias was John the Baptist's dad. An angel appeared to him and told him that he and his wife, Elizabeth, would have a son, even though they were beyond their childbearing years. Zacharias could not understand how that was possible. His response to the angel was somewhat shocking: "How can I know this for sure?" Asking for proof was foolish. As a result, he lost the ability to speak until after John was born. Perhaps it was God's way of not letting him destroy the miracle. More damage has been done through careless speech than probably any of us knows. As the Bible says, "Death and life are in the power of the tongue" (Proverbs 18:21).

The same angel showed up to speak to Mary, the chosen one, to tell her she would give birth to the Christ Child. She, too, had little understanding of how it could be possible since she was a virgin. But instead of asking for proof, she asked for understanding. The angel of the Lord responded to her kindly and gave her instructions about what lay directly ahead in her life.

We all lack understanding for some of life's greatest challenges. Trust in the One who is trustworthy is what makes these situations not only bearable, but a platform for personal advancement in our faith. While the Scriptures instruct us to pursue wisdom and understanding, the prevailing focus of the believer's life is trust. This is a most essential ingredient of our lives. There is no relationship with God without trust.

Some cultures exalt skepticism as a virtue. Their greatest fear is being gullible or misled. The fear of being wrong prevents them from ever really being right. Such a deception sells books to the fearful, but does little to shape the course of history through bold faith for the glory of God. Skepticism masquerades as wisdom and is applauded by those without experience. To maintain their own positions, they question the rights of others to continue moving forward. In some church cultures, this kind of approach to God is treasured, as scary as that seems. It is a self-affirming approach to the supernatural that basically denies God's involvement in the day-to-day issues of our lives. And anyone who seems to think that God actually cares about such things is quickly marked as delusional. This is a group that asks for proof.

To recognize personal need and ask for wisdom is a genuine virtue. This comes out of humility, which is the mandatory approach before the almighty God. Such a place of trust generally precedes the understanding being asked for. This childlike approach makes room for the God of the Bible to be the God of our everyday lives.

Most people pray, in one form or another. But sometimes those prayers are nothing more than demands made of God, telling Him how He should prove Himself so we know for sure; and without such evidence, we will not obey. God cannot be held hostage to our demands for action, no matter how strong we think the biblical promise might be. Being a follower of Jesus is not a contract with a business associate; it is a relationship with

God, who makes Himself known to those who seek Him. To seek the Lord is to seek His will, for we cannot want *the Lord* without wanting His rule. This is the heart of the yielded child of God. We long for understanding of mysteries, but at the same time, we embrace the privilege of obeying Him, regardless of how little we understand.

Prayer

Father, forgive me for all the times I tried to get You to prove Yourself before I was willing to obey. Please help me to hear clearly what Your will is, and give me the grace to obey boldly, even when I am fearful. I want You to receive all the glory for making this kind of lifestyle possible for me.

Confession

I will hold on to hope in every situation, for the God of all hope is my Father. I will no longer exalt skepticism; nor will I entertain the notion that unbelief is normal. I am a believing believer. And my new nature is one of great boldness and faith.

32

Hope

When Paul told us to prophesy
according to our faith, he
revealed why so many negative
prophetic words are released.

The Church should have the greatest hope, joy and love on
the planet. Such a people should enjoy life the most—living
in the pleasure of the Lord. Jesus accomplished all that was
necessary for us to live in this posture. That does not mean we
are a people without problems and challenges. We know that is
not correct. But in all things we are victorious in Christ. When
we lose hope for life, we are set up to view tomorrow with very
anemic faith.

I mentioned earlier the strange thing that has happened to
the heart and mind of the Church in this generation: Believers
have learned to become encouraged through bad news. Tragedy
and crises are the gauge by which the Church determines that
we are in the last days. And since the last days culminate in the
return of the Lord, tragedy becomes a source of encouragement.

It is often forgotten that the prophet who said "darkness
will cover the earth" also said "His glory will appear upon you.

Nations will come to your light, and kings to the brightness of your rising" (Isaiah 60:2–3). Those are statements of incredible hope and promise. And they far outweigh the darkness addressed in that chapter. The absence of hope often blinds our eyes to what Scripture says of our glorious future. The verses announcing difficulty are profoundly overshadowed by the verses of great promise, in the same way that light is superior to darkness.

When our mindsets are fixed on tragedy as a sign of the times, we become encouraged through such tragedy. When we apply that mindset to our approach to life, we see how our prophetic utterances are affected. It is possible for our faith to be aimed at the wrong target, which adversely affects the prophetic ministry. The result is that we declare truth about prevailing darkness in a situation, but we fail to speak the further revelation that could help change that situation. It is true that prophecy foretells the future, but it also plants seeds of change, creating hope and faith in the hearts of those who see God's intentions on the earth.

The profound implication of Paul's statement is that our faith influences what we prophesy. Declarations out of our faith affect the outcome of events.

Is it possible to become a people who, while not ignorant of the darkness in this world, live as the antidote? Is it possible for us to live aware of the devil's devices without becoming overly devil conscious? Is it possible to be so possessed with the promises of God that no matter what happens around us, we speak with the hope that Jesus made possible through His resurrection?

I believe it is. And I think it is time for all of us to heed Paul's cry to prophesy according to our faith. May our decrees come from *great* faith for all that Jesus provided.

Prayer

Father, please help me not to be ignorant of the devil's tricks and devices. But I also need help not to make that my focus. I want to be a person who carries promise into every situation. Help me always to be more impressed with Your answers and promises than any of the tragedies that happen in the world. By Your grace I purpose not to become simply a broadcaster of evil, but to live as a part of the answer for my generation. Help me to be a person of infectious hope.

Confession

Jesus is the reason for hope. He is my hope, my future and my victor. All things that pertain to life belong to me because of His accomplishments at Calvary. I refuse to be impressed with the devil. God's promises are greater than any conflict or challenge, be it personal or international. I am a person with ever-increasing hope, and I will speak accordingly.

33

Love

God does not look for worship; He looks for worshipers.

God is not an egotist in need of affirmation. He is not trying to help His approval ratings on planet earth and, therefore, commanding us to tell Him how good He is. God is quite secure in who He is. He does not look for worship. But He does look for worshipers. There is a difference.

Consider this: God is love. And love always chooses the best. He could want nothing better for us than for us to be worshipers because we always become like whatever we worship. There is nothing better that He could want for us than for us to become like Him. That is love, true love.

Genuine worship is a transformational experience. This is where the follower of Jesus encounters God, the glorious One. Certainly a part of that experience is our offering of thanksgiving and praise. That becomes the prelude. It is not the warm-ups, in the sense that it is the practice before the real game. Offering thanksgiving and praise is a wonderful part of our call as "priests unto the Lord." We have the distinct privilege of ministering to Him with these sacrifices. But God responds to our offerings. It is good to remember that fire, the manifest presence of Jesus in the Holy Spirit, always falls on sacrifice. In Psalm 22:3, we find the idea that God inhabits our praise. The picture becomes increasingly clear: As we minister to Him, we encounter Him. The only logical response to this encounter with the presence of God is worship.

The concept of worship as a transformational experience applies to the worship of false gods, too, whether in the form of self-promotion or an actual idol. In Psalm 115, the writer makes it clear that idols have eyes, but they cannot see, etc. And so it is with those who worship them. They lose the ability to see and discern right from wrong. They have become like what they worship.

As we encounter His glorious presence, we are changed. Changed from glory to glory. It is stated that "when He appears, we will be like Him, because we will see Him just as He is" (1 John 3:2). This statement refers to a future event. But the principle remains: Seeing Him changes us. Perhaps that is what the apostle Paul was talking about when he said, "But we all, with unveiled face, beholding as in a mirror the glory of the Lord, are being transformed into the same image from glory to glory, just as from the Lord, the Spirit" (2 Corinthians 3:18). Notice he says that we are transformed into the same glorious image of God that we behold, from glory to glory. We become like the one we worship. The point is that it is the glory that transforms a life more profoundly than anything else available to us as believers.

There is no greater privilege for the believer than to encounter His face. This is the ultimate call. And those who behold Him, in whatever measure He allows, are given the grace increasingly to become like Him.

Prayer

Heavenly Father, I thank You for the wonderful privilege of loving and worshiping You. Thank You that Jesus qualified me for this honor. Help me always to recognize You above the busyness and activities involved with my faith. My heart's desire is to honor You with all I am and to be like Your glorious Son, Jesus Christ. I ask these things that You may glorified.

Confession

Jesus qualified me as a priest unto God. I am welcomed into His glorious presence to minister to Him in the same way that Jesus is welcomed into His presence, for I am in Christ. I declare that God has predestined me to be like Jesus, and this privilege of worship is a part of His plan. So I live for God to be exalted in and through my life in all I am and all I do.

34

Faith

God's trust in us is measured by what He has entrusted to us.

When I make this statement, many people think I am referring to wealth, title or fame. I never bring those elements into the equation, for true wealth has little to do with those things. God's value system is quite different from ours as He looks at everything with eternity in mind. Besides, those things could never adequately reveal the greatness of His heart for us because they are all finite, and His love for us is infinite.

God's trust in us is seen in His gift to us, the great treasure of heaven—the Holy Spirit, who is the Spirit of Christ. And with His presence comes His name, His authority, His glory, His joy, His purpose, His destiny. This list of benefits is without end.

The Holy Spirit is so revered in heaven that Jesus warned us that blaspheming Him is to step into eternal judgment. While the Holy Spirit does not speak of Himself, both the Father and the Son speak of Him with great love, respect and celebration. And it is that Third Person of the Trinity who resides in us and rests upon us. How much does God trust us, and how much does He trust what He has done in us? Enough to give us the Holy Spirit, the treasure of heaven. That one thought alone could keep us in awe for all eternity.

Every aspect of the life of the believer is made successful or not according to our relationship with the Holy Spirit. Some make the mistake of speaking of the Holy Spirit as an "it." Tragically, for many He is not a person one can know and interact with. Such a mistake is costly. It is like starving to death while standing next to a refrigerator full of food. The answer to everything in life really has to do with our desire and willingness to listen to and be empowered by Him. Whether it refers to our personal lives or ministries, all is connected to the influence of this indwelling presence of God.

This is why any focus on *our* strength, *our* faith, *our* willingness to obey, *our* surrender, *our* motives is entirely wrong. Now, these things matter. They do. They really, really do. But when I am the focus, I am relying on my own strength. It is about me. It is about my perspective and extremely limited perception of what God has already accomplished for me. And nothing could be more boring or trite. But when He is the focus, there is strength for everything I am assigned to do.

I challenge you to consider how much God believes in you and what He has done in you. Put your faith where His is. I challenge you to start the journey of discovery of how much God really believes in what He has done for you. The answer is: Enough to entrust the revered One, the feared One, the fragile One (in all the right ways) to live within the being of every single follower of Jesus Christ. Shift the focus from yourself to Him, from your faith to His faith, from your understanding to His understanding, from your confidence to His confidence, and you will have endless courage to follow God's predetermined plan to make you successful in all things pertaining to His Kingdom.

Prayer

Father, You amaze me in every possible way. I need to see the way You do, which is not even possible without Your help. I want to see the profound nature of Your work on my behalf. I long to see why You are so confident in me, enough to entrust me with the Holy Spirit. Thank You that You have already set the stage for this to be answered. And let this answer be unto the glory of God!

Confession

I believe in the thorough work of Christ on the cross—it was for me. I believe the Father's perspectives can be mine. So I declare that the blood of Jesus qualified me for the Holy Spirit. I am qualified. I declare that the Holy Spirit qualified me for every good work modeled by Jesus. I am qualified. My confidence is in what God accomplished on my behalf. I will not dishonor Him by embracing fear above faith or turning my focus from Him to myself. My faith is alive, practical and looking for another expression today, that God may be glorified.

35

Hope

Sometimes our breakthroughs begin
when we refuse to be impressed
with the size of our problems.

It is common for me to go to a city and hear statistics about how few believers attend church on a weekly basis, or how many witch covens are within a 25-mile radius of the church, or how revival has not come to that city. It is common to hear how many pastors have quit serving in the area in order to go sell insurance or some other occupation besides ministry. It is way too normal to hear from people who need to be healed that they have been prayed for hundreds of times without any noticeable improvement, or that their disease gives them a less than 1 percent chance of survival, or that their sickness is rare.

This is a real tightrope for me, as I want people to be real and not pretend that something good has happened. Yet the fact remains: Many people are impressed by their problems. They live in reaction to the devil.

I do not mean that they are impressed in the sense of having admiration for the devil or for the issue in their lives. But they are impressed in the sense that the problem has left an imprint—an impression on their minds—over and above any promise from God or the revelation of His extremely benevolent nature. It is as though they speak self-fulfilling prophecy, as it becomes increasingly difficult for them to see breakthrough, while the same problem yields easily in the life of another who is not impressed with darkness. There is nothing wrong with an honest approach to a problem, but I am never impressed with the size of a problem if I have seen Him or His promises clearly.

I am convinced that some people do not want to be healed. Oh, they would like to be free from pain and affliction or doctor's bills. But the attention to their problems actually provides great emotional currency. The wrong kind of attention has the ability to fuel the problem, giving it a reason or license to remain. For some, the need for attention and sympathy far outweighs the need for anything else. It is a perversion, to be sure. But it is not as uncommon an attitude as one might suspect. Just about the time you sense they are breaking free from this way of thinking, they begin once more trying to convince you how serious the problem is or how rare a breakthrough is in that area. Strangely it is easier to feel good about not getting a breakthrough when the problem appears big. This weird approach is actually the evidence of unbelief.

Remember the old saying "A bird in the hand is worth two in the bush"? The attention I receive from the problem feels secure and stable. In this illustration it is the bird in the hand. The miracle of healing or deliverance is much harder to hope for, for then I face the possibility of disappointment. This is the two in the bush. The unrenewed mind values the security of sympathy now over the possibility of a miracle. For with sympathy, at least I know what to expect.

The drive to remain free from disappointment has given place to this hopelessness and perversion of Christianity.

Prayer

Father, I am in great need of seeing what You are like. I have spent way too much time being impressed with the size of my problems instead of being overwhelmed by Your greatness as seen through the promises of Your Word. Please increase the grace upon my life to behold You, clearly. You are all I want. I want to please You with every gaze of my heart. Please allow me the privilege of displaying Your greatness to those You have given me to touch with Your love. I ask these things, all for Your glory and honor.

Confession

By the grace given to me I declare that I will no longer live in reaction to the devil, but will instead live in response to God. His promises are great. He has thoroughly thought through everything I will face in my lifetime and has provided promises for every situation. I refuse to feed my soul on sympathy and pity. I refuse to allow my heart to settle for lesser things. God is a perfect Father to me, and I joyfully embrace His perfect will for my life.

36

Love

Jesus is building a community of
believers who can recognize the source
of a word they do not understand.

The most profound example of community in the Bible is
no doubt the new believers in Jerusalem after the outpouring of the Holy Spirit. This is found in the first few chap-
ters of Acts. Their love for each other was so powerful that
the Bible says they had no needs. All of their requirements for
food, housing and employment were met. My favorite part of
this story is that the sacrificial giving that took place in the
context of community was never commanded. It came out of
the love they had for God, which was illustrated in the love
they had for each other. This is a beautiful picture of love,
of community.

Jesus started this reality in the lives of the disciples. While
there is not a lot of information about how they took care of
these sorts of needs, we do see Him addressing everything from
self-promotion, giving and serving to preferring one another.
These are all subjects connected to community. It appears that
these twelve men, plus Jesus, lived in community as they traveled
around the country preaching the Gospel of the Kingdom. A

beachhead was established that exploded exponentially in the outpouring of the Holy Spirit.

I have pastored two different churches in my lifetime. Each of them had a mighty outpouring of the Holy Spirit. The first one came after I had pastored a group of people for about sixteen years. While there is always a certain measure of surprise and many questions whenever God shows up in powerful ways, the church remained intact throughout that season of great change. New wine is poured into new wineskins because stretching is involved.

When the outpouring of the Spirit came to the second church, it caused great upheaval. It started a month or two after my arrival as their new pastor. As a result, about a thousand people left the church, splitting it in half. What was the difference? In the first church, our relationships helped us weather the mysteries that an outpouring brings. In the second church, I was new and had not yet built the sense of community in which the bond of love would hold us together. Some very wonderful people left as a result.

Jesus was a popular speaker. People would go without food and travel great distances just to hear Him talk and perform the miracles that gave credibility to the message. But that popularity was brought into question one day. There were thousands of people present. Probably close to fifteen thousand people had gathered around Him. He had already multiplied food to feed them. He then decided to preach. His sermon topic was the most offensive of His career. He announced that the people had to eat His flesh and drink His blood to have any part with Him. The community of listeners was divided over His message. As a result, they fought and argued with one another.

A mass exodus ensued. Imagine speaking to thousands, watching them disperse until you are left with twelve disciples. You can imagine how the disciples felt. They were riding His popularity quite well, hoping He would soon become king. Their aspirations were quickly evaporating. He turned to His community, the Twelve, and stated that His words "are spirit," and that the Spirit gives life (John 6:63). In other words, what He had just taught the crowd was as full of the Holy Spirit as were the messages the crowds liked. He said only what He heard His Father say. But this time, the people did not understand what was spoken. In fact, they found His words offensive. While the disciples also failed to get the message, they did recognize that when Jesus spoke, they received life (see John 6:68).

In the context of community, there is grace to receive things from God that would be threatening otherwise. Love enables us to extract the richness of life that God intends to give us through a word we do not yet understand. That is a huge part of the life of the follower of Jesus. As someone once said, "God offends our minds to reveal our hearts." This was never truer than in John 6.

Prayer

Father God, I want to live in love as You designed it. Help me not to live in independence and call it obedience to You. I desperately want my love for You to be measured by my love for people, my sense of community. And in the context of community, help me to embrace those things You have brought my way that are designed for Your glory and for my benefit, even though I may not understand them completely. I trust You and give You praise.

Confession

I will live in love. I will live in community. My heart is set on glorifying God by how I value people. As a result, I have purposed not to react to the things I do not yet understand, but will seek for understanding in the context of my love for God and my love for people. I do these things for the glory of God.

37

Faith

One of my greatest joys is to
stand with faith-filled people. But
one of my greatest honors is to
stand in the midst of unbelief.

Just being in a room filled with faith is a joy beyond description. True faith is not burdensome or self-promoting. It does not need to prove itself. Instead, it gives overwhelming confidence in the ever-present goodness of God, the One who acts on behalf of His own.

It is one thing to see an individual with great faith; it is quite another to see the same from a company of people. This is rare indeed. But I believe it is about to become the norm. I am thankful to be able to say that this reality is increasing almost daily. As a result, the exploits that are done for the glory of God are staggering. This biblical mandate of faith is being lived out by a community of believers who have the same level of devotion to Christ. The variety of gifts and expressions creates the most beautiful tapestry I have ever seen. This is the privilege of living in a community of believing believers. But it seldom starts there.

Before there is a community of great faith, there must be a person who puts a stake in the ground and says, "I will live by faith regardless of how many people join me." Great movements usually start with one person who says he will follow God regardless of who else follows. He seeks to honor God in the way that pleases Him—with great faith. Tragically, I have heard good people state that they are waiting for a spouse to believe before they will pursue this God of the impossible. Others wait for family members or friends. Still others want their church elders to lead the way. Regardless of how sane that reasoning sounds, it is insane. The issue is not, Who should believe with us? It is, What will I do with the God-given moment before me? The grace to believe is a gift from God that must not be disregarded through delay. It is not a disposable commodity. It is a most precious gift from God.

While I will always prefer being able to stand in faith with the great company of believing believers, I embrace the moments when I am forced to stand alone. Those are the moments that shape us. They rid us of that dreadful fear of man that is so often given a virtuous name, such as *honor* or *wisdom*. In those moments we find out what really is in our heart of hearts.

A word of caution in order: Even though I cherish the moments to stand when others do not, these moments must never allow me to ignore the fact that I am still only one member of a very huge Body, and that accountability and honor matter.

Is it possible to stand in faith when those we are accountable to will not? Yes. Never lower your faith to those around you. Instead, demonstrate the authentic nature of your faith through the love and honor shown to those who question your wisdom and position. Remember, faith works through love (see Galatians 5:6). If my faith exists without love, it will be self-promoting and eventually self-destructive. Love never promotes itself. And neither does faith, when it works through love.

Prayer

Father, I thank You for all the moments You give me to honor You through faith, for You are truly the faithful One. Help me to embrace these moments without fear, and even accept that challenge to stand alone when it is needed. I know that the ability to believe when others turn away is not because of my greatness but is the product of Your grace. Thank You. I simply want to bring glory to You through Your wonderful gift of faith.

Confession

I love the privilege of standing with people of great faith. And I will treasure the moments when I find myself standing alone, believing when others have become fearful. The grace of God is more than enough for me in any and all situations, as I was created to bring God glory through who I am and all I do.

38

Hope

People with resentment attract people with complaints.

One of the great mysteries of life is how people with certain values, be they good or bad, attract others with the same values. I can assure you that if you put a person who loves gossip in a work environment with a hundred other workers, within a couple of weeks he will have attracted into his life those who gossip. It is a strange phenomenon, but completely true.

People who live bitter lives are puppets of the devil. They attract demonic chaos that brings distortion. Bitterness seldom exists without reasoning. So the evil one loves to provide the justification to remain bitter. What better way to sustain what is wrong than to immerse it in the atmosphere of justified resentment? And so the complainers are drawn into the lives of the bitter. When this happens, it is more than a natural law of like attracting like through mutual interest. It now becomes a spiritual law, where the internal values of the heart help to build alliances with the invisible world. In this case, the alliance is with the demonic. The bitterness and resentment is so vile that it contaminates entire groups of people in a very short period of time.

There were times when friends of mine heard evil report after evil report about someone, and I heard nothing, even though I was involved with the same circle of friends. I realize that there could be many reasons for this. But one that I am certain of is that when people become offended, they are more likely not to trust the ones who offended them. The one sure way to separate friends and to destroy the beauty of unity is to feed suspicion. The wrong attitudes in their hearts attract information that confirms what they have *discerned*, thus furthering the divide between those who should be illustrating love, mercy and unity. The heart is a beautiful thing, when protected. But it can be vile when the enemy is allowed to sow seeds of discord into it.

This truth can also work to our benefit, in that good standards of the heart actually attract the things needed to sustain those values. I have practiced this as though I were trying to learn to play a musical instrument or something requiring equal discipline. Here is an example. The continual hope in my life thrives on reports of what God is doing. When I value testimonies of God's wonder-working power, I attract those with stories of breakthrough. It is beautiful to watch. There are times when people almost line up to tell me stories of good news! The values of the heart attract the fuel needed to sustain those values. If hope and faith have a high priority on your list of values, watch as you attract people with great hope and faith who have faith-building stories.

It is wisdom to recognize what you attract into your world. Obviously, not everything that comes to you in life is because you attracted it. But it is fitting for us to become aware of unusual patterns—not for the purpose of shame or condemnation, but for the purpose of bringing about any needed life changes. Those patterns just might indicate something in our hearts that we have been blinded to. If it is gossip, turn away from it the next time it comes. If it is dirty jokes, learn to pull out of such conversations. Make it clear as to what you value if you are questioned. Reset the standard of what you are willing to listen to, and heaven will back up your commitment and make sure you get a steady diet of things eternal.

Prayer

Heavenly Father, please give me the grace for my heart to overflow with Your values. I want to attract into my life what pleases You. That is my cry. But I also need You to show me the things I might be ignorant of that displease You and bring difficulties into my life. My greatest desire is that You be glorified by who I am and how I live. Thank You for the promises You have given me that help me maintain hope in all situations.

Confession

I will protect my heart from the seeds of resentment and bitterness. By God's grace I will keep away from these things, and will give myself to those things that please God. As a result I am now a person of great hope. And my hope is secure in the goodness of God, all for His glory.

39

Love

Some listen to learn; others listen to critique.

The Bible states that love "believes all things" (1 Corinthians 13:7). God was obviously not making room for foolishness or being gullible about things that are not true. That would contradict the rest of Scripture. So what does He mean in that statement? He is describing the heart condition necessary to grow and receive from the various gifts (people) that He has placed in our lives. Some of those people are hard to receive from for a variety of reasons. And sometimes we, not they, are the problem.

Occasionally, we cannot hear truth from certain people because their mannerisms are different from what we believe is appropriate. They might be boisterous and loud or quiet and subtle. Either can appear wrong if our background experiences differ from theirs. This is generally more of a cultural issue than a spiritual one, but we do not always know the difference. Fearing error, we build walls of protection, but sometimes protection meant to keep us safe from error makes us a law unto ourselves.

Sometimes people speak great truths, but their terminology means something different to them than it does to us. This is called semantics. A word or phrase might mean something positive to them, but be a "trigger word" for us. Those who listen to learn can decipher this confusion, but those who listen to critique have a heyday mocking the "error" of sincere believers. The absence of love in listening keeps them from insight, and, worse yet, they dishonor servants of the Lord.

I am not alone in witnessing the devilish reactions of many people who confess to be followers of Jesus. I do not question their faith. But their religious zeal takes over their character and they slander a person they might actually agree with if they took the time to communicate. If they were in relationship and saw how that particular truth was lived out on a daily basis, they might become friends for life. Being a self-appointed policeman for the Body of Christ is a nauseating task.

Love is the answer. Love positions us to succeed. When I am in community with a group of people, love is a priority. Love puts me in a place of listening to understand before making a conclusion. And even if I conclude that I strongly disagree with someone, my love forbids me to reject and mock that one in my zeal for truth.

Love truly wins because love believes all things. It looks for the best in an effort to understand. Those who need always to be right become an offense even to the people who agree with them. Love tempers. It softens. It makes diversity more than tolerable. In love, diversity is necessary to give a true expression of the Body of Christ to this world. When we love only those we agree with, we are doing nothing more than any other service club in our community. God expects and requires more. That is why love believes all things.

Prayer

Heavenly Father, please help me to be a better listener than I am a talker. I really want to understand the heart of the people You have connected me with. And I really need help so that I am not quick to judge and criticize people with whom I differ. Thank You that You have made us different from each other by design. Help me to value this diversity and never oppose what You have made. I want my love for people who differ from me to be the very thing that brings You glory.

Confession

I am committed to a life of love in the context of community. I am also devoted to a lifestyle that celebrates diversity. In my quest for truth, I will not dishonor persons made in the image of God. Instead, I will listen, eager to learn and eager to understand. I acknowledge that this is the way of love, and I will live this way for the glory of God.

40

Faith

The hungry crave;
the satisfied evaluate.

I once sat in a restaurant close to a very unhappy woman. Her unhappiness had to do with the meal she had ordered. Her steak was not hot enough. She had the server take it back and bring it back hotter. She was also dissatisfied with the second attempt. The third time the manager himself brought a brand-new steak to her. When she said she did not like that one either, he explained that he had brought it straight from the fire to her table. She was determined to complain, as the fire, itself, was not hot enough.

Those who become the most demanding of their meals are usually the ones who are the farthest away from hunger. Satisfaction breeds a certain sense of snobbery in our attempt to enjoy perfection. And while such high standards may be acceptable when you are paying for an expensive meal, the concept often speaks to the conditions found in much of the Church. Those with the most options often become the most demanding. Many choose the church to attend on a given weekend by who is preaching that day, or by the sermon topic. Only the spiritually full have such options.

Hunger is an interesting phenomenon. It moves people to do strange things. Stealing is forbidden in Scripture, for instance, but Solomon seemed to show sympathy to the thief whose stealing is motivated by hunger. And even though the thief must repay what he has stolen, Solomon said that the man is not despised in his community (see Proverbs 6:30). Unusual behavior is more excusable when a person is hungry.

Spiritually hungry people often show similar traits. Protocol seems to fly out the window for those with extreme hunger for God. I have watched shy people become loud, timid people become aggressive and the complacent become extremely bold in their faith. It is beautiful. It is one thing that is certain to bring fulfillment of the Hebrews 11:6 definition of faith: "He is a rewarder of those who seek Him." Hannah lived out of this same reality when she appeared drunk before the priest, but was actually intoxicated with a desperate prayer for a child (see 1 Samuel 1:13). Eli understood and excused her bizarre behavior brought on by hunger.

This kind of hunger comes out of the conviction of the goodness of God, who gives good gifts to His children. It exists because people believe He keeps His promises. People seldom come to this conclusion through Bible study alone. In the end, it requires diligent pursuit of what the Bible reveals. It would not be an exaggeration to call this hunger a "burning within." It is ignited by God, but sustained through the cooperation of the individual.

The satisfied evaluate. They usually evaluate other people's experience, teaching, and their confession and hope. Sadly, some people would have no ministry at all if they could not critique and criticize others. They are not known for what they believe; they are known for what they oppose. They have no history of igniting or sowing into moves of God. Instead, they are known for critiquing the "meal" that others enjoy. They remind me of restaurant critics who cannot cook.

Faith has such a different approach to truth. Yes, deception is a concern, and, yes, the devil exists. But faith expressed in hunger is much more convinced of God's goodness and His promise to satisfy than it is of the devil's ability to steal, kill and destroy. The hungry become preoccupied by the One. He is available to those who pursue with reckless abandon. He comes with the ability to keep them safe. At the center of this kind of faith is humility, for it causes a person to "lean into" a situation, expecting God to speak and give direction. Faith anticipates good because God is good. Faith with hunger is more gullible than suspicious.

Prayer

Father, please help me always to be thankful for what You have given me, but also always hungry for more. I do not want to fall into critiquing other people's experiences at the expense of going deeper with You in my own walk. Please surround me with people who inspire me to hunger for more, and may my life have the same effect on others.

Confession

I was designed to walk in faith and humility. I am able to do this because God is good, and He gave me the gift of hunger. For this reason, I will pursue the One who has promised to be found by me!

41

Hope

When God gives us a promise instead
of an answer, it reveals His desire to
draw us into our eternal purposes.

I have heard people say that God needs us. This simply is not
true. He needs nothing. He is and has been completely self-
sufficient for all eternity. But we have been on His mind forever.
And those thoughts have been for our welfare and blessing, and
not our calamity. His ideas for us are good, incredibly good.
He has great dreams for us, just as any good Father has for His
children. He told Jeremiah that He knew him before he was
born. God was so involved in His dream for that prophet that
He *experienced* him, before he was. That is intense dreaming,
the kind that God is very capable of.

The all-sufficient One prefers partnership in which His brilliance and beauty are seen in those who worship Him by choice.
As our hearts are set on Him, we are changed from glory to glory.
Yet we are also the object of His desire—we are His dream come
true. He longs for those who want to learn to display His heart
and ways, to become co-laborers in establishing His Kingdom
and bringing glory to His name. How is it possible not to be
possessed by hope when God is our Father? Impossible!

The Father has such longing for partnership that He sometimes responds to our cries in ways we misunderstand. We look at the problem; He looks at the big picture. We look for intervention; He looks for sons and daughters to look, act and live like His Son, Jesus. He desires for us to live in the authority of power that Jesus lived in. Do you think that if God answers every prayer for us, fixing every problem we pray about, that this personal transformation will ever happen to us? No. We will remain like the infants in the home whose every need is cared for. In that environment, all we have to do is cry to get the needed attention. He wants more from us. For us to grow up, we must attack the problems at hand with the mind of Christ, exercising the power and authority given to us in His name. Maturity means we live and think responsibly. Jesus must be *re*-presented in our generation.

There are times when He gives us promises instead of answers. He wants our involvement in becoming mature believers that *re*-present Him well. Embracing His process gives us the privilege of being a part of His answer. He wants more than to see someone healed or delivered; He wants to work through us. He wants His people to demonstrate His heart for humanity and become a part of the answer—bringing His healing, deliverance and overall spirit of breakthrough to each unique situation.

When He answers a prayer for us, our job is quite simple: Watch Him work and give thanks. He works on our behalf in ways that impress us so deeply that we celebrate His intervention with great joy. When He answers prayers through us, our job is much different. This time, our response to His leading is the key to the breakthrough. Jesus said, "I only do what I see my Father doing." The Father showed Jesus what to do to bring about the miracle. Such co-laboring is still in God's heart today, and He wants a Bride that is fully developed into maturity for His Son.

Prayer

Father, You amaze me. You amaze me in the way You desire for me to be able to illustrate Your heart to the world around me. I live with hope because of this. Please help me to recognize when and how You are moving in a situation so I do not miss my God-given opportunities to see Your Kingdom come. I need wisdom to know when the cry of my heart is being answered for me or answered through me. In advance, I thank You for both.

Confession

By the grace of God given to me, I will be faithful to cry out for breakthrough, but not be afraid of using His name to help bring it about. My heart longs for God to be glorified in and through me; therefore, I embrace, with joy, His longing to work His purposes in and through me that the world might know what He is like. I do this that His name might be exalted in all the earth!

42

Love

We often celebrate the ones
who humble themselves under
the mighty hand of God, but
despise the ones He exalts.

We have a theology for humility. And rightly so. Jesus both taught it and displayed it. We have room for those who lay down their lives for others day after day, living sacrificially for the sake of the Gospel. We often celebrate them when they are in that position.

But what happens if God does what He says He will do in their lives? The apostle Peter declared, "Therefore humble yourselves under the mighty hand of God, that He may exalt you at the proper time" (1 Peter 5:6). We have a theology for humility, but we lack one for blessing and promotion. Is it possible for God to exalt people, also for the sake of the Gospel? I obviously do not mean into positions of pride and independence. But I do mean positions that allow them to influence the mind molders of this world. Until we can settle some of these issues of the heart, we will never step fully into our purposes.

One of the reasons this subject is so hard for the people of God is an issue that none of us wants to own up to—jealousy. Straying from love leads us right into this sin. It is a cancer that devours the heart and can cause otherwise good people to fall under the spell of their own judgment of others. In order for this evil trait to exist in the heart of a believer, we have to give it a noble name. *Discernment, intercessory burden* and *God told me . . .* are all expressions used to give this destructive influence a hiding place. Let's face it: It is challenging to watch someone else get what you have been working and praying for, or at least desiring in your heart.

Once again, the apostle Paul teaches us: "Love . . . is not jealous . . . does not seek its own" (1 Corinthians 13:4–5). Until you can celebrate and take part in the promotion of another, you cannot be certain that you are free from the influence of jealousy. The enemy works hard at stirring up this feeling, as it disqualifies so many from their own destinies. And the powers of darkness fear our coming into our destinies.

Self-promotion is a destructive influence, especially in ministry. *Does not seek its own* is addressing this issue. God is interested in our promotion. In fact, He is more interested than we are. But when we advance through self-promotion, we have to continue to promote ourselves to keep the position. It is exhausting. And it leads to jealousy. We must repent of it the moment we see it.

Learning how to celebrate the promotion of another is often the prerequisite to our own promotions. It is called stewarding another person's possessions. When we do well with what belongs to another, God makes sure that we receive what belongs to us. This is part of the reason we are called to rejoice with those who rejoice and weep with those who weep. We must temper our own hearts that we might partner with the experience of the others we are with for their benefit.

Prayer

Father, help me to celebrate the promotion of Your children the way You do. Help me to see Your hand in their promotions so I do not fall for the trick of fighting Your will for their lives. I want only the advancement in my own life that You deem me ready for, knowing that too much at the wrong time could affect my passion to please You in everything. I pray these things that You may be glorified in all the earth.

Confession

God exalts people at the proper time. He is the only One who knows what the proper time looks like. Because I love the will of God, I position myself with readiness to honor those whom God is honoring. I do this that the name of Jesus will be held in highest honor in all the earth.

43

Faith

Our minds are either renewed or at war with God.

Because the renewed mind is of such great importance to God, I think it is safe to say that all of God's dealings with His people have, in some way, the renewing of the mind as a primary target. We know that faith does not come from the mind; it comes from the heart. Yet the renewed mind enhances faith. It gives faith a context for divine reasoning.

The framework for the renewed mind is the nature and promises of God. Living aware of and out of that reality is how the renewed mind is shaped. The renewed mind, for example, honestly sees the potential for a child's lunch to feed a multitude.

This kind of thinking does not come easily. The disciples struggled with it—and they saw the unlimited display of God's goodness flowing through Jesus every day. Yet they still struggled with believing that having no more than one loaf of bread in their boat was okay for the journey (see Mark 8:14). And that embarrassing reaction followed two occasions when they saw small amounts of food multiply to feed large crowds.

The word *repent* means "to change the way we think." This is not a mind-over-matter issue. If that were true, then only the highly disciplined could repent. Repentance is a gift from God. It is godly sorrow over sin that enables a person to shift her perspective on reality—the superior reality. Repentance is seeing from God's perspective.

This, then, gives us a clue about the renewed mind: It is the way of repentance. Either I see from God's perspective, or I need to repent. "The mind set on the flesh is death, but the mind set on the Spirit is life and peace, because the mind set on the flesh is hostile toward God" (Romans 8:6–7). The mindset of the flesh is death, and it is hostile toward God. There is no middle ground, thus the need for the Holy Spirit's work in the renewing of our minds.

Because repentance is often thought of as self-abasement and self-criticism, many miss their chances at the renewed mind. They get too caught up in themselves, as though becoming introspective could bring about a transformed way of thinking. In reality, introspection robs people of their moments in God to truly see as He sees. Even when God is convicting us of sin, we hope in His mercy. In other words, we must at some point shift our focus from our failure to His ability and desire to forgive.

The really sobering part of this equation is that the unrenewed mind is at war with God. Hostile toward God, it is incapable of producing good fruit. Simply realizing that truth helps us to produce the much needed "godly sorrow." Without it, there is no repentance.

If you are prone to fall into self-criticism as an expression of your sorrow over sin, quickly recognize that even that posture must be repented of. Somehow we must learn to see the error of our ways without making it all about us. Only as we see the surpassing greatness of His love and mercy for us will we be able to see clearly what He convicts us of without falling into the trap of self-centeredness in the name of repentance.

Prayer

Help me to see clearly. Help me to stop limiting You to what seems reasonable to me. I want to see through Your eyes and live from Your nature and promises. Thank You for settling every issue ahead of time at Calvary that I might believe for the best because You are good. Thank You for Your unending goodness!

Confession

My mind is being renewed by God's unending grace. I am being changed from glory to glory, all because God is good and is fully committed to my transformation. I am confident that He will complete what He started.

44

The Church's obsession with avoiding
disappointment has given the seat
of honor to the spirit of unbelief.

Hope is one of the most important Christlike attitudes and
values we can have in this life. It must be nurtured continuously if we are truly to discover His heart. Without hope,
it is impossible to live life to its potential. God does not require
blind hope, in the sense that it has no reason for being. Nor is
this brand of hope mere positive thinking, pretending "all is
well with the world" when all is not well. In reality, this hope
is the joyful anticipation of good. It comes from discovering
His nature of perfect goodness by encountering Him and His
perfect promises.

Hope is anchored in the revelation of God's goodness and
bubbles up from our hearts in a way that affects our perspectives, attitudes and countenances. Since His goodness is the
greatest absolute in existence, it is what our hearts must be
tethered to for us to remain unwavering in this Kingdom reality called hope.

As I pastor, I know this challenge well. We often become
fearful of creating expectations that might go unfulfilled. And

there is not a decent pastor on the planet who wants to frustrate God's people with more unfulfilled promises. We face impossible situations almost on a daily basis—and none more difficult than standing with family and friends who face a great tragedy and ask why. As a result, I often hear pastors expressing concern about creating hope that will only go unfulfilled—again.

I understand the reasoning, in that we have often been left to help pick up the pieces of broken and unfulfilled lives. Hype in ministry is one of the biggest culprits. It is really good at creating expectations it is incapable of fulfilling. None of us wants to be involved in that fruitless activity. But trying to compensate for that abuse by embracing the absence of hope is absolute foolishness. It becomes a self-fulfilling prophecy—we get exactly what we expect: nothing. Protecting ourselves from disappointment is ultimately embracing unbelief.

Many of us have been given an impossible assignment: to make sense out of a crisis or tragedy. While answers are often sought, they seldom help, at least not immediately. It is the heart that is hurting, not the brain. And while we try hard to offer comfort, the only real answer is the peace that passes understanding. Generally, we have to give up our right to understand in order to get that kind of peace. Putting it practically, we must become friends who love, serve, refuse to judge or condemn, all while carrying an unwavering trust in the goodness of God. People who have experienced great loss might question everything we believe and stand for. But as friends, we stay true to the revealed nature of God's goodness, while staying in a loving role that brings comfort and peace to those in crisis. That position brings such safety into their world that eventually peace becomes their possession forever.

I have watched as many try to insulate themselves from disappointment. That is an expensive choice, as they have to remove all sense of hope in order to be successful. It is a disastrous way to live. Where there is no hope, you will not find faith.

I remember several years ago one of the young men in our church was called to be a possible juror in an upcoming trial. While waiting in the room with a hundred or so potential jurors, he noticed a man in a wheelchair. He went to him and asked if he could pray for him to be healed.

The man's response was honest, asking, "What if I don't get healed?"

Our young man responded, "What if you do?"

That simple shift in focus helped this gentleman return to hope. Within moments, he was out of his wheelchair giving thanks for his miracle. Hope is the beginning of the life of miracles, for it joyfully anticipates our perfect heavenly Father to display who He is—in, to and through us.

Prayer

Heavenly Father, with Your help, I will not protect my heart from possible disappointment. Instead, I will give myself to protect what I know of Your goodness and always believe for the best. Your Word anchors my heart in the reality of what Jesus has accomplished for me. By Your grace, I will display this hope in an infectious way, that others will place their hope in the wonderful name of Jesus.

Confession

Just as I have given myself to live in love, I have devoted my life to being filled with hope. Jesus is the reason for such hope, which makes my hope stable and glorious. I will live this way so that God will be glorified and so that people will find salvation in the name of Jesus. And by God's grace, I will face each day with the joyful anticipation of good—God's goodness revealed.

45

Love

Passionless leaders cost everyone who follows them.

One of the more sobering truths in Scripture is the discovery that our mistakes and sins never affect only us. The greater the responsibility in a person's life, the greater the impact on those who follow behind. This is an inescapable truth. And it does not help to say each person is responsible for his or her own choices, as though the fallen leader has no responsibility. It happens. And it has consequences. This principle applies to everyone though, not just those with a title. (It is also important to note that the costly right decisions by a leader release great benefit to those who follow. It works both ways.)

This issue applies to much more than moral failure, as tragic as that is. It applies to how a person leads. Parents, take note here as well, as true leaders are not just those with titles. There is a great story in the Bible about Elisha and a king (see 2 Kings 13:14–25). Through a series of events, Elisha was at a place to define the destiny of King Joash and the impact of his leadership on the nation, but he needed to put his heart to a test. Elisha asked the king to strike the ground with arrows. Joash did so, but struck the ground only three times.

Elisha became angry, saying that if only he had struck the ground five or six times, Israel would have annihilated her enemy. But now Israel would have only three temporary victories. Think about it. Israel, as a whole nation, was destined to have three temporary victories over an enemy because the king responded without passion to the prophet's command with the arrows. Token obedience is disobedience.

The issue at hand is love. Real love is not casual, and it is not convenient. It is very disruptive in nature. A person who falls in love loses all sense of focus and seems to abandon his usual priorities. This love is measured by the word *passion*, which is that fiery burning of the heart for another. The believer should have this kind of heart for God. It is called our *first love*.

This love is evident in the way we relate to people. When Jesus cleared the Temple, His disciples remembered the Scripture that says zeal for His Father's house would consume Him (see John 2:17). We are that house! Jesus' passion is aimed at the house of God, His people. Are we to be any different? Our passion is recognized by the way we approach our God-given assignments in life. Everything we do is to be unto the Lord. We all have arrows in our hands, and others are watching what we do with them. My intent here is not to promote fear of man or raise an unhealthy awareness of responsibility. But neither do I want us to ignore the fact we affect people's lives in a profound way.

The hardest test we face is not the one we know we are taking. When someone tells me he is being tested by God, I want to tell him, "It's an open book test—those are the easy ones!" The hardest tests by far are the ones we face, but never even realize it was a test until it is over. Such was the case for this king. If you are anything like me, you wonder why the prophet did not tell him it was a test. I would be asking to take the test over because now I know what he is looking for. The problem is, though, the prophet already found what he was looking for. He found what was in the king's heart without prodding and preparation.

I have to admit that I have not always done well with these kinds of tests. In school, I was really good at studying hard right before the test, but did poorly if I did not know in advance what was required. This is not a heaven or hell issue. It is a test to see how much of what we have asked for we can handle without it destroying us.

The good news is that our passion helps to ignite the hearts of others. The people who look to you for direction or inspiration are powerfully affected by your simple act of striking the ground with the arrows. Living in love with zeal for His house is the privilege of every follower of Jesus. Strike the ground until those around you come into their greatest victories!

Prayer

Heavenly Father, I know I need Your help once again. I want to live this life with passion. But I cannot fake it. I need You to show me Your heart for Your house. I need to see Your eyes of fire that are focused on me, not for my destruction, but to ignite my heart to burn like Yours. This is my desire, that I might honor You in ways I have yet to discover. These things I pray for the glory of God.

Confession

My heart burns for God. I know that this is more than mere enthusiasm and shallow zeal. My heart burns for Him because His heart burns for me. I love Him because He loved me first! At best, I can only mirror what He has in His heart. And it is to this end that I commit my life—to display the passion of God.

46

Faith

Faith is evident in the act of obedience.

One of the traps I fell into as a young man was thinking that to be great in God, I needed to measure my faith. I read the stories of the great men and women of God of the past and longed for the same place of significance and impact that they had on the course of history. Although I wanted significance, it was significance from God's perspective, not man's. It had nothing to do with fame or a big name. God knows who truly trusts Him. That is what drove me.

All the heroes of the past were people of great faith. It became obvious rather quickly that to have the same impact as they did, I would have to have similar faith, as that was the one absolute ingredient for pleasing God. So I tried to measure my faith and looked inward to do so. But whenever I opened that *jar of faith* to see what was inside, whatever was there quickly evaporated. I never seemed to be able to find it when I was looking for it.

Conversely, there were times when I knew that God had commanded me to do something that I did not think I had the faith to do. Instead of going into self-examination, I just obeyed. I will never forget my moment of discovery when I felt as though God spoke this to me: *You couldn't have obeyed without faith.* I had been looking in the wrong place. Greatness was not found by looking for greatness. Neither was faith found by looking for faith. It was found in yielding to His will and purposes. From that point on I have made obedience the focus instead of measuring my faith stores.

Faith is the result of surrender, not determination. Faith is the normal response of a believer toward the One who is perfectly faithful. That being said, obedience then becomes the most practical way to discover the faith in a person's life.

Today I have many heroes of the faith. They are highly respected worldwide for their faith and their exploits. I know many of them personally, and each one stands out in my world for extreme obedience. I say *extreme* because they look for opportunities to trust God for the impossible. Being with them helps me. But being with them also makes me nervous, for they reset the standard of what I call the *normal Christian life.* Because of their influence on my life, I cannot stay the same.

Nothing of eternal significance is discovered by looking inward. Looking God-ward is quite the opposite, however. Favor, life, faith and everything else of importance are unveiled in that one glance. Readying myself to do whatever He says to do next is my great privilege and responsibility. And perhaps strangely to some, it is what reveals the actual measure of faith that I live by.

Obedience is the expression of authentic faith, for obedience is what illustrates trust, as all relationships are founded on trust. A moment of learning to respond to His voice will do more to develop my faith than a thousand years of looking inward.

I love and need simplicity. Having only one gauge on my dashboard, *the heart to obey God gauge,* makes this life of trust much easier. By grace I can do this one.

Prayer

Father God, You are trustworthy beyond all imagination. And I honor You for that. Please help me to anchor my heart and mind in Your trustworthiness, because I always want to be found trusting You. I do not want my quest for faith to be tripped up by introspection, so please help me to be aware of those moments when I am prone to fall into the trap of thinking it is about me. Thank You in advance for the grace to live as You have designed me to live—full of faith and completely faithful.

Confession

I was designed to trust God, naturally. It is not complicated to be given the task to trust the most trustworthy One in existence. And this I will do with great pleasure all the days of my life, for the glory of God.

47

Jesus is returning for a bride whose body is in equal proportion to her head.

The return of Jesus Christ for His Church will be one of the most wonderful moments in all of time. As such, it is called the blessed hope. But what is He returning for? A divided Church that is a jigsaw puzzle He has to put together in heaven? Is He returning for a weak, anemic Bride who needs hospital care before the wedding? Or is He returning for a Bride who has made herself ready? Fully ready. Mature and glorious.

I grew up in a church culture that held the conviction that things would get worse and worse in the last days, and then Jesus would return. While I never remember my dad teaching that, it was the Pentecostal culture we lived in. As a result, Jesus' return amounted to a rescue of His Bride before the devil deceived and destroyed all her members. There are certainly verses that seem to imply that outcome, if you are predisposed to see them.

I remember when I bought my first new car, a beautiful blue Toyota Corolla Fastback. That was in 1978. It had five-speed transmission, air-conditioning and a cassette player; everything a guy could want. It was so exciting to get something that nice, something brand new. My wife and I and our two little boys fit perfectly into this gift from God.

Then I began to see something I had never noticed before: There were many Toyota Corolla Fastbacks in the world. Now that I had one of my own, my eyes seemed trained to spot what had apparently been there all the time. As one who had a vested interest in that brand of car, I quickly noticed them everywhere. Internal values can enable you to see what you did not see before. The opposite is also true. Internal values can blind you to what has been there all the time. This is especially true of reading the Scriptures.

The question we must ask ourselves is, Are my values shaped by His values? When we study the last days, we are prone to come up with all sorts of interpretations. The biggest problem with our last days' theology comes from our study of the last days. I know that sounds strange, but is it really legal to study that subject separate from the overall theme of Scriptures? Is it a unique point of theology that can be divorced from the redemptive work of Jesus in making us new creations?

But what happens when we study God's purpose for the Church, or the thorough success of saving grace, or His promise and purpose for planet earth? When the study of the last days defines our overall theology for life, we are allowing the abstract to interpret the obvious. Our interpretations of the symbolic items in Scripture, such as the beast, the seven seals, the seven years and other endless mysteries, shape the things that are obvious. Is the study of those things wrong? Of course not. They have a place. But it is dangerous to allow the abstract to redefine what we know to be true. Jesus did not save us only to save us again.

This quote is actually mixing metaphors, which is often dangerous. I do it in this case to illustrate the combined realities: We are members of His Body, and also His Bride. As members of His

Body, He is the head. As the Bride, we are what He will return for. We would cringe at the thought of an infant's body trying to hold up an adult-sized head. Yet that picture represents all too well the theology of many. Why is that important? If we do not expect to end victoriously, we will always create a theology that allows for failures and shortcomings and ultimately the misrepresentation of the ministry of Jesus on earth. We do not need a theology that empowers weakness and failure. The work of Christ at the cross was sufficient in its ability to present us faultless and victorious—triumphant in both purity and power! Jesus is returning for a bride whose body is in equal proportion to her head. The victor will return for the victorious one. The King of glory will return for the glorious one. That is why His return is called *the blessed hope*!

Prayer

Dear Father, I want to live life on this earth in a way that honors You—a life of great joy and delight. But I also want to maintain my longing for Your Son's return. Please help me to keep my affections pure and established in Your purposes for this life. It is my desire to reign in life in a way that turns people to You through the overwhelming revelation of Your goodness.

Confession

God is my source for all things pertaining to life and godliness. It is my privilege to live from the great victorious triumph of the resurrection of Jesus, that God's nature would be discovered by people all around me. I will do this by the grace given to me, for God's glory.

48

Love

Christianity was never meant to
be recognized by its disciplines,
but by its passions.

For me, it is a tragedy when the Gospel is recognized by discipline and form and not real passion. I believe in structure. But structure should contain something. We know that the Bible talks about new wine being put into new wineskins so that as it expands, the skins will stretch. Make no mistake, the treasure is not the skin; the treasure is the wine. The structure is important because of what it holds. Discipline holds and gives value to the real treasure—love, as seen through passion.

A disciplined life is vital for us to come into our full potential. It is hard to read the epistles and come to any other conclusion. I think it can be said that real passion helps develop great discipline. There is probably no better example than to watch a man and woman who have fallen in love. You never have to tell them to think about each other. You never have to tell them to sacrifice for the other's benefit. Neither do you have to suggest that they put aside other interests so they can spend time together. Those things happen automatically, which tells us we will do much more naturally when we are in love than we could ever do through effort because it is required. Passion/love forms the best discipline because it comes out of the heart, and it dictates easily how life will be lived.

The church of Ephesus lost sight of this very kind of love—first love. They were known for so many good things. But the one thing they were supposed to maintain above everything else was this first-love relationship with God. Repentance was the necessary step, but that repentance had to take on an unusual form to lead to true restoration. God told them, "Remember . . . repent . . . do the deeds you did at first" (Revelation 2:5).

Sometimes our lives get so busy with spiritual activities that we lose sight of why we are alive, and what God has assigned us to do. Priorities get rearranged simply because of pressure, and our passion gets replaced with duty. God commands, "Remember!" Memory can be an invaluable tool in helping us to recover lost territory in God. Stop everything and remember what you used to feel, think and live like.

He follows that with the command, "Repent!" Confess and turn from any lifestyle that compromises a life of passion for Jesus.

I find His next command the most interesting: "Do the deeds you did at first." If this word were spoken to a husband and wife who needed to fall in love again, it would look like this: Buy her flowers. Call her from work on your break. Think of ways to bring her delight. Plan surprises for her that will make her happy that you two get to spend your life together. That list is fairly obvious—and the wife has an equal list—but you get the point.

Now transfer that to your first love for Jesus. How much did you talk about Him? What was your prayer life like? What was it like to pour yourself into reading the Bible for the first time? What were the kinds of things you would talk to God about? These are all *first deeds*. He is not saying you need to earn His love; He is leading you into action that can reactivate the passions of your heart simply through obedience. The nature to love Him with reckless abandon is still in you. By doing what you used to do, you are calling that nature of passion back to the surface, so that it might once again dictate to you how life is to be lived.

There are few things in life more beautiful than an older couple still in love. They have aged gracefully together, enjoying the gift they have been given. And that gift is each other. Such is the life of a seasoned saint who is still living with first-love passion for the Lord and Savior, Jesus Christ.

Prayer

Heavenly Father, help me never to become stale in my love for Jesus. I want to display simple passion that brings You great honor. You have done so much for me that I cannot imagine living any other way than completely for Your glory.

Confession

I love God with all of my heart. My heart burns with affection for the One who loved me first. And it is my honor to be a passionate lover of God every day of my life. I will do this for the glory of God.

49

Faith

In the absence of faith comes disobedience.

Two absolutes are required of the follower of Jesus: love and faith. Love is the greatest manifestation of being a disciple of Jesus: "They'll know you are My disciples by your love" and "The greatest of these is love." But faith is also an absolute, as the writer of Hebrews declares: "Without faith, it is impossible to please God." Paul joined the two uniquely in His statement in Galatians 5:6: What matters is "faith working through love."

Too many believers talk themselves into unbelief by treating faith as a rare commodity that only a few very special folks can attain to. I did that for many years. Whenever I tried to strive for faith, it ended in disaster. Relegating the life of faith to the giants of yesteryear seemed like the only logical response. But I could never settle that issue in my heart—something just did not seem right. When I realized that faith does not grow by striving, but rather comes through surrender, then I saw it was for me, too.

In making faith unattainable, we elevate the expected life of the believer to such a high place that it is out of reach for the common man. And if Jesus stood for anything, He stood to bring the extraordinary into the reach of the one considered common. His twelve disciples were not the elite of His day. On the contrary, they were common, sometimes embarrassingly so.

It would be cruel for God to require faith from His children, yet make it unattainable. He is not that way. But neither do we enter a life of faith through self-will and selfish determination. It is entirely through surrender, surrender to His will, His heart, His nature and His promises.

Paul wrote the most challenging statement in this regard: "Whatever is not from faith is sin" (Romans 14:23). Once again, if faith is unattainable, God has destined us for sin. This obviously is not the case, as every person has been given a measure of faith. It is a gift from God that enables us to succeed. This is the mercy of God for each one of us. He requires something from us, and then provides that something for us. It is like a teacher requiring you to pass a test in order to graduate, and then giving you the answers. Yes, He is that good.

It comes down to the use of our wills. Will we yield ourselves to His purposes and express the natural fruit of surrender, or will we go our own way and walk in unbelief? In the absence of faith are sin, disobedience and everything that stands against the purposes of God for us.

Prayer

Father, I start this day by declaring my surrender: I surrender to Your will, Your heart, Your mind. Everything about You fascinates me and draws me into the pleasure of serving You. Help me to keep this life of faith simple, as You have given me the answers to the test You want me to pass. I celebrate You for Your ongoing kindness toward me.

Confession

Faith has been given to me as a gift. It is something I possess simply because God willed it so. And I confess and declare that it is my honor in life to demonstrate His faithfulness through my faith. I accept this privilege that God may be honored in all the earth!

50

Hope

Hope is the soil that faith grows in.

Promises give hope. In fact, the entire Gospel of the Kingdom of God is an ongoing promise that gives hope to all its citizens. Page after page of the New Testament gives us reason to anticipate the extraordinary invasion of God into the impossible situations in life. The Gospel is called the Good News for that very reason. It certainly works in eternity, but the wonderful news is that it also works in the here and now.

The word *hope* should not be connected to the common concept of *wish*. Hope is not a long shot, the idea that perhaps something good might happen if we get lucky. Hope is just the opposite. It actually means "the joyful anticipation of good." My wife's parents used to film her and her siblings on Christmas morning when they were getting ready to come into the living room to open their gifts. The movie camera and its extremely bright lights were set up facing the hall where the children were bouncing off the walls with excitement. They were waiting for Dad to say, "Merry Christmas!" They knew something good was about to happen, and they were already happy about it, even though "it" had not happened yet. Their excitement was verbal, physical and emotional. There was no guessing about their mental condition. The fact that they were filled with hope was profoundly clear to anyone who saw them. This is one of the best examples I know to illustrate the true meaning of this powerful word: *Hope! The joyful anticipation of good.*

Living without hope is really a wasted life. We were born and designed to live with great hope. Of course, this does not eliminate problems or difficulties. We still have to learn to deal with disappointment. That stuff happens to everyone. But hope is greater. Hope is the soil that faith grows in. Faith takes aim at specific situations; hope is general. It is the overall confidence in God's desire, commitment and ability to make all things work for good.

Show me someone with great hope, and I will show you someone who is positioned to move in great faith. Hope is the byproduct of what I think about, meditate on and fill my heart with. Promises help to create great hope. If I am facing any kind of problem, and I do not have a promise for it, I will be ill-equipped to face it, and I will fall far short of what was possible. When we feast on His promises, we are having intentional impact on the measure of hope we will live and abide in.

Show me someone who ignores the mandate to live with hope, and I will show you someone whose faith does not measure up to the size of the challenge he faces over and over again. This is a serious issue. Hope needs to be in place long before an opportunity to use it arises. This is what enables us to have an immediate response to those things that challenge us. Today's hope is the soil of tomorrow's victory of faith.

Prayer

Dear heavenly Father, please help me to recognize the promises You have planted all throughout my life, just for me. I do not want to be ignorant of those things. Help me to live full of hope, and may this heart condition be contagious, that You might be glorified.

Confession

God has made it possible for me to live in hope continuously. He has given me promises ahead of time so that I have an answer for whatever comes my way. My life was thoroughly considered and planned for, long before I was born. The great Designer designed me for hope. And I will live with hope, unto the glory of God.

51

Love

You have reason to question anything
you think you know about God that
you cannot find in the Person of Jesus.

Who among the followers of Jesus would suggest that the
sacrifice of animals could atone for our sins? None! Who
among us would promote a pilgrimage to the Temple every year
to have the priests mediate between God and ourselves? Not
one of us! Do you know anyone who would tell the terminally
ill that they are unclean, and that they need to announce their
presence when they walk down the street?

No one who is a true believer would endorse such practices.
Yet do you realize that many Christians actually do similar
things? This happens every time we allow Old Testament standards to trump the revelation that we find in Jesus Christ for
dealing with sickness and evil. Are we any different when we see
Jesus heal all who were oppressed by the devil in Scripture, yet
explain that God afflicts people with disease in order to build
their character? No. That is an appalling practice.

Jesus came to an orphaned planet to reveal the Father, the
Father who is Love. God had never been adequately revealed
before as the Father. Jesus came for that purpose. Everything

Jesus said and did had that one primary focus: to reveal the Father. Everything before Jesus served a different purpose: to reveal the lost condition of humanity and point to the only possible solution, Jesus Christ the Redeemer. The Law became the tutor that led people to Jesus as the only answer. In that sense, the Law and the prophets are glorious and absolutely perfect. But their time of application was then, not now. It is a mystery to me why people opt for Law that exposes us, instead of embracing the Good News Jesus came to reveal.

Another surprise for me personally is how many believers get angry with those who give their all to follow Jesus. Instead of looking to Jesus' example, they point to John the Baptist or Elijah or even Moses. These men were all perfect for their day. But Jesus came to fulfill what they all lived for. He came to reveal what they could not—a Father who loves people and paid the price for their redemption through the sacrifice of His Son. It is the greatest news ever. And it does not need to be muddied by what many call a "balanced" message—a little bit of Law and a little bit of grace. Jesus Christ is the message. He is the Good News. It does not get better than that. It is not too good to be true. It is so good it is true.

When you look for God's hand in world affairs, look to see what Jesus did with world leaders. When you want to see if God caused a natural disaster, look to see what Jesus did with storms. If you are trying to figure out if it is God's will for someone to be healed, look at Jesus' dealings with people in need. How many people did He turn away because it was not His will to heal? Jesus Christ really is perfect theology.

This piece of writing does not answer as many questions as it raises. I do not write this to provide answers as much as I do to set direction of thought and intent. In all construction, the foundation must be solid and straight. If we are not level at the beginning, we will be off by a mile the taller the building gets.

Prayer

Heavenly Father, I give You thanks for the whole Bible. Everything in it is priceless to me. Please give me the wisdom to recognize what I need to understand from the past in order to appreciate fully what You are saying to me now. I recognize Your Son as the way, the only way, to come to You as my Father. Thank You for that. I pray for the grace to illustrate His life well, for Your glory.

Confession

I believe the Bible is God's Word, and that all of it is profitable for my instruction. I believe that while the Old Testament is useful for instruction, its message must never trump what Jesus said, practiced and modeled for us to follow. I believe that Jesus Christ came to reveal the Father, and that He reveals Him perfectly. Now it is my turn. As the Father sent Jesus, Jesus now sends me.

52

Faith

Faith does not deny that a problem
exists; it denies it a place of influence.

I am grieved at how often I see believers try to *will* themselves
into faith, as though faith were a product of their effort.
Faith is not a choice; it is a fruit. An apple tree will bear apples
if it is healthy and abides in a healthy environment. There is no
fight. There is no travail. Nothing. It just happens as the natural
result of its nature and environment.

We are believers. That is our nature. Our sins have been forgiven, and we have received the nature of Jesus as our own. It is
in our nature to believe in the same way that it was in the nature
of Jesus to believe. We cannot create faith, but we can hinder its
creation by living contrary to who God says we are. Abiding in
Christ is the answer to more things than we can possibly imagine.

Sometimes, when believers are afraid of appearing weak
through unbelief, it becomes a fight for them to prove they have
great faith. The problem is that faith does not become evident
through such means. It does not parade itself. It is not self-promoting and does not need to prove itself. Faith is born out of rest,
not striving. It is the basis upon which we face impossibilities.

When people strive to prove their faith, they often deny that a problem exists, because having a problem seems like a sign of unbelief. That is not true. Jesus acknowledged when a problem existed. So did the apostle Paul and other writers of Scripture. In fact, all the heroes of the faith recognized when they were facing something that had no natural solution. The key is not to give it a place of influence. We do not live in reaction to darkness; we live in response to God.

Other times people do not deny their problems, but carry them in their minds all day long. Some call this an *intercessory burden*. Most of the time, God calls it *worry*. True intercession acknowledges the weight of the problem, yet is ignited by the promises in God's Word. The two realms are held in tension until the problem gives way. (Some problems have personalities behind them that must be dealt with.)

My wife will carry a problem before the Father and ask, "So what are we doing about this?" She is looking for His heart, His lead. When she gets it, she goes forth in His authority to administer His will in the earth. This basically means we carry the problem only long enough to gain the Father's heart on the matter. We never carry it to the point of becoming impressed by the size of the problem. That would be living from the problem toward life, instead of living from God toward the problem.

Work to cultivate an awareness of the heart of God for all that concerns you. You will never be impressed by the size of a problem again.

Prayer

Father, please forgive me for wanting to make sure everyone around me was aware of the enormity of my problems. I am sorry for making them bigger in my heart than my awareness of You. Help me live from Your heart toward life. Help me live impressed only by You. I ask that You help me hold the name of Jesus in highest honor.

Confession

I am a believing believer. It is my nature to believe God. I refuse to be impressed by the accomplishments or threats that come from the powers of darkness. All those powers and plans have already been defeated by the resurrected Christ, who lives in me. I am alive for the glory of God.

53

Hope

Any area of our lives for which
we have no hope is under
the influence of a lie.

God is a perfect Father. He has unlimited resources that He puts at our disposal to complete our assignments. He also possesses the ability to look into the future and see what is coming our way. He never commands us to do something and then leaves us helpless to find our way in His assignment. His grace is His enabling presence. It is fascinating to me that He commands me to do something, and as I yield to His commands, He actually performs His work through me. It is Jesus in me who makes the impossible possible.

He is diligent, faithful and wise. He is perfect love, beauty and wonder in everything He is and does. As such, He is the ultimate Father who goes to great lengths to equip us today for our tomorrows. He has thoroughly considered our abilities in light of His purposes for our lives. He took our weaknesses and failures into consideration when He called us. None of our successes or failures, weaknesses or strengths surprises Him. Each was already calculated into His overall plan for us and for the earth. He is the ultimate steward of all He possesses—everything belongs to Him. It is all at His disposal to enable this mysterious co-laboring partnership we have with Him to accomplish everything He has purposed. None of it is earned. It is all by grace. God did not leave us without all the tools necessary to live in victory. One of the most essential tools in our toolbox is His promises. Living conscious of our promises from Him enables us to live in hope. It is up to us to pursue the God of the "Promised Land" to give us what we will need for the next season of life. Not that we have to beg; it is already His idea and in His heart for us. But the importance of hungering for His Kingdom, while maintaining a heart that is poor in spirit, cannot be overemphasized. This condition of heart attracts the unlimited resources of God.

Having said all of that, it comes down to this. Every problem I am facing, He has already considered ahead of time and has given me the tools to face victoriously. We were designed to reign in life. But the enemy has worked to cause fear, intimidation and anxiety that we might lose sight of the tools that God has given us. That hopelessness renders us nearly powerless, which is the great contradiction as we have been given access to all power.

I like to look at this issue of promises this way: It is as though God has gone into my future and brought back what is necessary to get me there. And those are His promises.

Knowing God as a loving Father, the only One capable of preparing us ahead of time for all that life dishes out, is to establish us in life in great overall confidence. This is hope. We must be unwilling to live without hope in any area of life. We do not rely on our greatness, significance or even great faith. We rely on a perfect Father who has thought of everything.

Prayer

Heavenly Father, thank You for receiving me so completely into Your family. Thank You for Your total devotion to my present and my future. Please help me never to lose hope for any part of my life. Point out any carelessness that still exists in my thinking, or in my perception of You as my Father. I ask for all of this that I might represent Your Son, Jesus, well. And may all of this bring You glory. Great glory!

Confession

My Father is perfect in every way. He leaves nothing unattended, nor is He careless about my life. I have reason for great hope because the great hope-giver is my Father. I will guard my heart from the lies and distractions the enemy brings. I purpose to be able to say with Jesus, "Satan has nothing in me!" I do these things that I might present my life to God as an offering for His glory.

54

Love

God's ability to use sickness for His
glory does not mean He approves
of sickness, any more than God's
ability to use sin for His glory
means He approves of sin.

A constant discovery throughout our walk with the Lord
Jesus Christ is what love looks like. He always chooses
the best for us because that is what love does.

God's ability to use bad things for His glory has caused
some to think that He is the author of those bad things. This
belief usually gets swept under that mysterious carpet called
God's sovereignty. While I love and delight in the wonder of
our sovereign God, I am grieved at how much in our lives is
inconsistent with Jesus' life, yet gets labeled as God's mysterious will.

God is sovereign. That is an absolutely beautiful truth, one
beyond comprehension. But is it legal to put things that Jesus
never tolerated into that category and call it God's will? May
it never be! I certainly want to be careful in this subject. But
I also want to be Christlike, which means to be like Jesus. He

did not allow much that we allow. People often read the gospels stories about His miracles for encouragement, but not as an example to follow.

Is God able to use sin? Yes. Absolutely yes. Solomon was David's son. God loved Solomon and ordained that he be king of Israel. The David/Solomon era was the *golden age* of Israel's history. Yet Solomon's mom was Bathsheba. David married her after their adulterous affair that led to the murder of her husband, Uriah. That was sin to the max! Yet our sovereign God was able to take such horrific actions by David and produce one of Israel's greatest kings. Were David's adultery and act of murder God's will? No. God does not violate His own law to accomplish His purposes. But as I like to say, God is able to win with a pair of twos, meaning He can turn any situation into a winning hand. He is God.

Is God able to use sickness? Yes! I have seen it countless times. Families come together to rally around their dying loved one, and reconciliation comes to broken relationships. Often people who are void of any thought of God begin to seek godly counsel. And still others start to pray. It is very beautiful to behold. It all comes from a big God, one full of great love, one who is willing and able to use any situation for His glory and our benefit. But to call sickness His will is to credit Him with the devil's work.

I quoted this verse earlier, but look again at how it sums up this point so beautifully:

> "You know of Jesus of Nazareth, how God anointed Him with the Holy Spirit and with power, and how He went about doing good and healing all who were oppressed by the devil, for God was with Him."
>
> Acts 10:38

Jesus is God's will illustrated. He went about doing good. That good was described as healing and deliverance. He did those things because God was with Him. The presence of God on a life means certain outcomes are expected. Healing and deliverance are two of those anticipated outcomes. This is what love does.

God is good. The devil is bad. Health and healing are good. Sickness and disease are bad. It's not complicated.

Prayer

Heavenly Father, I give You thanks and praise for Your ability to use anything for Your glory and for our benefit. You amaze me for You are so wonderful. Help me not to become so careless in my thinking that I attribute to You the devil's work. But also help me never to lose sight of Your hand in less than ideal circumstances.

Confession

God is good, always good. God is also eternally big, and He is able to redeem any situation for His glory. By God's grace, I will never credit Him with the devil's work. Instead, I will set my heart to behold God's redeeming love in the most impossible situations. I will do these things to the glory of God.

55

Faith

Faith brings answers, but enduring faith brings answers with character.

¹

One of the most exciting parts of the life of the believer is seeing prayers answered. And the more impossible the problem, the more memorable and impacting is the answer. Answers to prayer are the wonderful privilege of the follower of Jesus. They are the products of co-laboring with God, an honor that is beyond comprehension.

God answers prayers differently for each person and each occasion. But if we fail to understand how He moves, we can wind up frustrated in the midst of a potentially massive breakthrough. Believers often abort the answer they have prayed for because they are ignorant of how God moves.

I wish we could see how often God answers our prayers the moment we pray—but answers in seed form instead of the full-grown answer we are looking for. We cry out for a major breakthrough, and instead God provides the seed for that breakthrough. We ask for the oak tree; He gives us the acorn. The tree is in the seed. Seeing that truth will change everything about how we pray, and how we steward the moments we have in God. God created seeds, and seeds grow with proper care. It is His way.

Sometimes our greatest need is the *answer*, and sometimes we actually need the *process* that brings the answer. We want sudden intervention; He wants the answer to be safely planted in the life of the yielded believer. His intervention is sustained through the personal development of the one who does the praying. In other words, He wants the answer to have a safe home in the life of a believer who has learned the ways of the King.

Often we are praying for the right things, but if the answers were given all at once they would actually destroy our lives. For that reason, enduring faith is important to God.

When we learn the art of focused, unending prayer, our hearts are strengthened in the same way that isometrics develop our muscles. Character becomes the *muscle* that is developed during the time of waiting for an answer while persisting in focused prayer. Waiting that is sure of the answer is what develops character in the life of the disciple of Jesus.

Answers to prayer are great. Answers to prayer that come with growing character are even greater. God is always looking at the big picture. The fact that we are in His picture should amaze us all.

Prayer

Father, help me to steward well the moments You give me. I do not want to miss the seed of an answer You provide for me—or miss seeing it develop into the thing my heart cries for. I want strength of heart to be formed in me, all for Your glory.

Confession

I was designed to get answers to prayer. I accept the fact that answers come in different forms. Acorns grow into oak trees, and I embrace the opportunity to see small answers develop into the full-blown answers I long for. I was created for this purpose: that God might be glorified.

56

Hope

Living in regret will become your biggest regret.

E very moment I spend in regret robs me of time to have an impact on the present and sow into my future. Getting us to live in regret is a clear trick of the devil, as it lessens our effectiveness in the now. Ultimately, he uses this trick to get us to question indirectly the true effect of the blood of Jesus and to remove us from ever seeing the full impact of our faith.

Regret is sneaky. Most of the time it exists because of our desire to live a life that is fully pleasing to the Lord. It feeds off the conscience. That is how it has permission to remain. The conscience is a wonderful gift from God, but its usefulness comes from being under the influence of the Holy Spirit. And the Holy Spirit never removes our pasts from under the blood of Jesus for reexamination.

I doubt that there is a person living who could not think of many things he wishes he had handled differently. My list is long. The more I ponder those things, the more I give place to a cloud that positions itself over my head, distorting my emotions and thoughts. Hope is infected by an atmosphere of regret. Imagine yourself standing downwind from a campfire.

Your clothing and hair would smell like smoke, long after you had left the campfire. In the same way, regret is the smoke that saturates all we put our hands to do. Regret leaves a stench that only repentance can remove. We must learn to recognize it as an enemy and fight it accordingly.

Regret robs us of hope. It disqualifies us, in the sense that we become dislodged. Picture an arm that is dislocated, out of joint. It is still alive, and very much a part of the body, but it has little function. Movement is severely restricted by terrible pain. Regret is similar. The memories of past issues bring great pain to the person who has lost sight of the transformational work of the blood of Jesus. I have watched people lose hope by their focus on the past, even though they had repented and confessed their sins. It seemed as though they were living in regret, hoping to convince themselves that they were truly sorry for sin.

When this happens, regret propels us into the task of trying to earn forgiveness. You cannot earn a gift; otherwise, it has become a wage. Forgiveness is a wonderful gift from God. And that gift positions us for the incredible promise regarding the things we would love to change: "We know that God causes all things to work together for good to those who love God, to those who are called according to His purpose" (Romans 8:28).

God is able to use the worst circumstance of our lives for His glory. This is something that I cannot comprehend, but know it is true. He is the master craftsman, able to take what we might consider rubbish and turn it into a masterpiece. This is the glorious work of a perfectly loving Father who has purposed to do these things for each of us.

Prayer

Dear heavenly Father, I need Your constant help to look at my life the way You do. I cannot afford to look at my past in a way that displeases You or causes me to become ineffective in the life You have assigned for me. Please give me Your ability to look even at failures with great confidence in Your commitment to make those things work for Your glory and my benefit. I trust You for these things and give You praise!

Confession

God has forgiven me; therefore, I forgive myself. I will not accuse someone He is not accusing, even if I am that someone. My forgiveness is for His glory. Regret will no longer be a part of my life. I will not give away my future to the enemy of my soul, who wants to tie me to my past. I have been set free. And I will live in Jesus' freedom for the glory of God.

57

Love

It is not possible to achieve true
greatness in the Kingdom without
valuing the greatness of another.

I still cannot get over the picture of the King of kings putting
a towel over His arm to wash His disciples' feet. It is an absolutely stunning example of humility. Humility is Kingdom; pride
is at the root of everything evil. But the pursuit of greatness is
not necessarily evil. In fact, it seems that those who spent time
with Jesus had latent desires awakened in them regarding their
own significance. As a result Jesus never rebuked His disciples
for their desire for greatness. He simply redefined it by pointing to a child.

Look again at one of my favorite verses on this topic: "Therefore humble yourselves under the mighty hand of God, that
He may exalt you at the proper time" (1 Peter 5:6). The phrase
under the hand could be a frightening picture to someone raised
in an abusive home. But when we realize that we are putting
ourselves under the hand of a perfect, loving Father, we see
what a privileged opportunity we have. This hand is a hand of
covering and protection.

The *humility* part of the equation is fine for most of us. At least, the concept is acceptable, even though at times it is hard to do. What is difficult for us to handle is God's response to our humility: "that He may exalt you." What do we do with that? Many of us squirm or say things to undermine the honor given to us. Yet if we do not know how to receive honor correctly, we will have no crown to throw at His feet.

But an even greater challenge comes when honor is given to someone else. Many believers fail to understand God's process and try to undermine that promotion, exposing it as illegitimate. Some cultures call this the "tall poppy syndrome." If one poppy is taller than the others, that poppy is the one you cut down. This is a tragic and regular occurrence in some church cultures, under the name of humility, of course. This is in direct opposition to love. The Bible says humble *yourselves*, not make sure everyone around you stays humble.

I despise self-promotion. It aborts the divine opportunity for God's promotion and replaces it with its counterfeit. The believer spoils his or her own moment in God in an effort to be credited, recognized or honored. It is sad. Yet if I am not careful, I will allow my dislike of self-promotion to ruin my opportunity to recognize God's promotion of another, celebrating the one He celebrates. We never want to be found critiquing the one He is honoring.

The bottom line is that we are quick to endorse a theology of humility, but not one of blessing, nor of greatness. Perhaps we recognize the notion that "the greater position one has in life, the more spiritual that person is" is, in fact, a lie. But reaction to error usually creates another error. As a result, the Church is much more comfortable with poverty as a sign of spirituality than wealth. Neither is true.

The problem is not that someone receives a blessing; the problem is that we are skewed in our ability to maintain humility while God promotes and exalts, and then we project our struggles onto the lives of the people we watch get promoted around us.

Consider the meaning of this word *exalt*: "to lift up or to make great." Here is one of the definitions given to us from one of great reference works (Thayer Greek Lexicon) used in studying New Testament language of the word *exalt*: "to raise to the very summit of opulence and prosperity." That is about as far away from our understanding of the Gospel message as can be. Yet it is biblically sound and true. Sometimes the Bible's statements are so magnificent that we tend to think God must be talking about when we get to heaven. But that would be a very poor interpretation of this verse. It is speaking of now. Love has no problem believing this because it thrives on seeing others blessed by God.

I realize that the Internet does not always accurately reveal what is happening in the Church, but it can provide a glimpse. Let me illustrate something that I have noticed for the last several years. When God promotes people in unusually obvious ways, many in the Body take it upon themselves to warn of these dangerous *tall poppies*. If, for example, a believer writes a good book that sells a few thousand copies, there is no problem. People will usually leave that author alone. But let it sell millions of copies, and countless people create websites and YouTube videos to announce that the book is heresy. Jealousy is a cruel taskmaster. It distorts reality and robs us of an opportunity to join with God in celebrating one of His own. Those are priceless opportunities that we must embrace and steward well.

When God blesses us, we need to maintain and increase the measure of humility that got us to that place. Blessing does not position us to build our own kingdoms. It simply increases our responsibility to use His favor for the sake of others. It is how this Kingdom grows in impact and influence.

Prayer

Heavenly Father, I need Your constant help on this so that I do not undermine Your work in people's lives. It amazes me that You would want to honor anyone. But I celebrate that. Help me to be free from the suspicion that ruins so many good people's lives, and help me to see whom You are exalting. I want to bless whom and what You are blessing. My heart's desire is for You to be highly exalted through all of this.

Confession

I will celebrate the one God celebrates without the need to point out his or her weaknesses or faults. I will bless what He is blessing and use the favor given to me for the benefit of others. God has made His grace available to me that I might succeed at this, all for His glory.

58

Faith

Miracles are often on the other side of inconvenience.

The life of miracles is joyful, exiting and frustrating. It is joyful and exciting for all the obvious reasons: People are set free, and Jesus' name is exalted! It is frustrating because miracles attract into your life people who need a miracle, and not everyone who comes leaves with what he or she came for.

That absence of a miracle presents us with two options: One, I can become satisfied with the absence of the miracle or, two, I can look for solutions, answers and understanding so I can learn to become more effective in this life that Jesus called me into. I chose the latter, which means I am always in school.

One of the more sobering lessons in this journey is seeing how often people pray, expecting God to come to them and bring the miracle. There is certainly biblical precedent for this expectation. But if we read the accounts of Jesus' miracle ministry with an open heart, we will notice that not one miracle happened the same exact way as another. And sometimes there was an action required before the miracle happened. Sometimes the action was required of Jesus, like spitting on a blind man's eyes and laying His hands on him (see Mark 8:23). And sometimes an action was required of the person wanting to be healed, such as directing another blind man to go and wash in the pool of Siloam (see John 9:6). Think about that story for a moment. Does it seem a little odd for Jesus to send a blind man to the pool of Siloam—or anywhere for that matter? He cannot see! The journey could not have been easy for him. And while sometimes people were healed as they went, this man was not. His healing came only after he washed in the pool as he was instructed.

As we read the accounts of Jesus' miracles, we see that sometimes Jesus brought the miracle to the people, and sometimes the people had to do something to get what they needed. And while we can say their action never qualified them to earn the miracle, we can say that their obedience positioned them for it. The trip to the pool would certainly qualify as an inconvenience for a blind man. But it was required for this man to be healed. And to keep things in perspective, it was not a cruel test from God mocking a blind man. Everything Jesus did was out of wisdom. In this case, wisdom was demonstrated in the assignment.

On another occasion, Jesus spoke with a woman about the miracle her daughter needed (see Mark 7:24–30). As Jesus was sent to minister to the Jews first, this Syrophoenician woman did not qualify for a miracle at that time. Her moment of inconvenience was not in performing a particular action, but in overcoming an offense.

Jesus told her that it was not right to take the children's bread and throw it to the dogs. Wow, that seems harsh! Churches have split for far less an offense than that. But throughout Jesus' interactions with Gentiles, we see that even though their season did not come until after His resurrection, He was always moved when faith was present in their hearts. In some ways, that is probably how He knew what the Father was doing—He recognized a gift from the Father operating in the lives of Gentiles. At any rate, He put a hurdle between the woman and her requested miracle. If she made it over the hurdle of offense, she would be positioned for the miracle. She did. And Jesus made special note of her extraordinary faith.

This is the bottom line: Thinking that God must come to us without any requirements can be one of the most arrogant approaches to God we can have. Much of what we cry out for in life is on the other side of inconvenience. Learning to get over offenses or learning to take bold actions is sometimes what is required of us to be positioned correctly for the miracle. It is time to hear and see what He is doing so that we do not miss our opportunities for breakthrough.

Prayer

Father God, help me not to think I have the right to demand that You do things my way. I know Your heart is already for me. So please help me to stay away from the fears and anxieties that cloud my ability to hear from You. I receive Your peace and Your promise, and I acknowledge that You are with me for the sake of triumph and victory that was obtained for me in Christ. Thank You in advance for my victorious breakthrough!

Confession

God's heart is for me, not against me. I declare that Jesus' blood paid for everything, and that I am positioned for the breakthroughs, signs, wonders and miracles that I need. I confess that God has given me the ability to hear His voice. So I set my heart to be a hearer of the Word that I might step fully into all that God has prepared for me.

59

When Jesus announced there would
be wars and rumors of wars, He
was not giving us a promise. He was
describing the conditions into which
He was sending His last days' army.

We noted earlier that many in this present time have been brainwashed into seeing only evil, expecting evil to increase and then taking comfort in the promised return of the Lord. While His return will be greater than anyone could possibly hope for, it was never meant to be a rescue mission. Plus, does anyone really think that Jesus would send us out with a mission that could not succeed or into a future with no hope? That is inconsistent with everything else we see in Jesus' commands and commissions.

Jesus foretold many things, including disasters that would strike the earth. He pulled no punches, so to speak. He also let His disciples know that if He suffered persecution, so would they. That is just a logical part of the overall equation. If religious leaders did not like Jesus, neither would they like those who imitate and follow Him.

I have yet to see anyone put this promise of persecution on his or her refrigerator. It does not fit among the promises we prefer to read every day. Yet Jesus would sometimes put this kind of promise right next to the ones that I might call "the good ones." Like the time He told His disciples that they would receive one hundred times more than they had given up to follow Him—and would receive it in this life. Then He added, *along with persecutions* (see Mark 10:28–30). I think He did that so we could not put the *hundred times more blessings* into the Millennium. We tend to take the best stuff, for which we have little to no faith, and put it into something for which we have even less understanding—the Millennium.

The commission Jesus gave to every one of His followers gives us insight into why He announced the coming calamities and difficulties. His commission was for us to pray and serve in a way that this world would become like heaven: in values, presence and purpose. He did just that when ministering to people. He once said if He cast out devils, the Kingdom of God had come upon that person (see Matthew 12:28). In other words, His world overpowered all that was wrong with this one He was delivering. It seriously was the invasion of the superior over the inferior. Darkness yields every time.

Our commission is the same. Jesus passed on His assignment to us, with the exception of His atoning death: Only Jesus, the righteous Lamb of God, the eternal Son of God, was capable of that one. Even if I am very poor at my God-given assignment, I cannot change it to something I am good at so I can feel better about my life. I am not in this to feel better about my life. Feeling good about my assignment, my giftings and my fruitfulness is not my pursuit. His will is. And in that process, I am fulfilled.

Wars, calamities and natural disasters are our assignment. If we are sent into them, then we can expect to be used by Him to bring His redemptive influence, as well as His peace, presence and power. It is much like a football coach telling his team what the other team will try to do to get them out of sync with what they know how to do. We used to call it *hearing footsteps*. When a wide receiver goes to catch a pass, the defender wants him to lose sight of the ball and hear only his footsteps, representing the fact he is about to be hit. In the same way, the powers of darkness want us to hear footsteps and take our eyes off the ball.

In reaction, Jesus said we have all authority and power from heaven to accomplish our assignment. The wars and rumors of wars? Footsteps. We have the ball.

Prayer

Heavenly Father, I love Your promises and Your plans for our lives and for this world. You are good, and all of Your plans are good. Thanks for letting me be a part. I really want to fulfill my purpose in this life and not be distracted by the things that are so easily distracting. Help me never to be impressed with the devil's plans. And help me to live entirely for Your purposes to be accomplished on earth, and for You to be glorified forever.

Confession

When Jesus announced that He had all authority and that we were sent into the world for the great harvest of souls, He was declaring He has the ball. By God's grace, I will never be impressed with the devil's plans as he does not have the ball. I embrace the purposes of God for my life, that He might be glorified forever.

60

Love

Sometimes our love for God is evident in what we hate.

If there is love, there must be hate. To love everything, even the things that destroy what we love, is not love. It is passivism. To be without emotion and tolerate everything in the name of love is not love at all. This could be compared to parents allowing a neighbor to come and abuse their children while they watch. They cannot rightfully claim to love their children. Instead, they are guilty of living without emotion and the responsibility to manage it well.

If someone threatened my wife, and I stood by saying that God would use all things for His glory and did nothing, you would have a right to question my love for my wife, as well as my sanity. Love is protective in nature. If there is a cancerous growth on the skin, we have the doctor cut it off. Why? Because we hate what could possibly threaten our health and even our very lives. This is love. It hates.

The psalmist wrote these words hundreds of years ago: "Hate evil, you who love the LORD" (Psalm 97:10). Please notice that even in the Old Testament, the command was not to hate people. That would be an illegitimate expression of this

189

mandate. God loves people. God hates evil. Evil destroys the people that God loves.

As believers, we are sometimes afraid of emotions, especially negative ones. Yet the Bible teaches us to be angry but not sin (see Ephesians 4:26). The climate of our day has made this a challenging command. That climate is summed up in the phrase *political correctness*. It basically means that we adjust our values according to what is popular and deemed correct by the media and/or those in charge; otherwise, we might cause offense. It is strange to watch this happen in society. People operating under political correctness are willing to offend 40 percent of the population in order not to offend the 3 percent that has gained politically correct status. In the fear of violating political correctness, nations around the world are inviting their greatest threat to take the place of honor in their cities, all in the name of *not offending someone*. Political correctness is vile as it replaces a value-driven culture with a fear-driven culture. The fear of man is at the root of this issue.

One of the better statements to come to the forefront in recent years is, "Love the sinner but hate the sin." This is a time when such a value must take center stage, for it carries the love/hate combination with great clarity. As a skilled surgeon carefully uses a scalpel, so must we be careful to hate evil only and not hate people. In fact, God's heart for people is extreme!

Perhaps the greatest verse in the Bible is, "For God so loved the world, that He gave His only begotten Son, that whosoever believes in Him shall not perish, but have eternal life" (John 3:16). God's love is sacrificial. Love must be seen in giving. And what is given is not what is deserved. Jesus taught us that to give someone what he has earned is really nothing special. But when we give in opposition to the judgment he deserves, then we have really loved well and given accordingly. This amazing truth is held alongside the contrast of hating sin. And it is this amazing love that reveals the kindness of God and leads people to repentance.

Prayer

Heavenly Father, I know You hate evil. I do not want to slip into the spirit of the day and lose my passion for all things right. But I also do not want to fall into the trap of hating people, even evil people. Please help me to represent You well by loving and giving to people long before they could earn it. I set my heart toward this privilege, that You might be glorified.

Confession

I was designed to love God, love people and hate evil. I will not partner with the spirit of the day and lose my perspective on the heart of God, and then become tolerant of the very things that rob people of life. I set my heart on this for the glory of God.

61

Most of what you need in life will
be brought to you. But most of what
you want, you will have to go get.

One of the frequent mistakes I see people make in the realm of miracles is waiting for God to come to them. They say, "God knows I'm hungry for revival. If He wants me to have it, He knows my address." Or the more common, "Why should I have to travel to that city or visit that church? God is here, too. If it's His will for us to have a great move of God, He knows we're willing." Some of these things sound spiritual but are actually very arrogant. It is foolish for us to think we can require God to pursue us. As someone once said, wise men still travel.

Lest you misunderstand, all of us are saved because God pursued us. There is no question about that. Did we find Jesus? Perhaps. But only after He found us and made Himself known to us. Certain things will be brought to us throughout our lives, but without an honest pursuit of God and all He has for us, it is impossible to fulfill our purposes and destinies. Some things can be discovered only by those willing to be inconvenienced with risk. Alongside the promises of complete and full supply are the commands to "Ask and keep on asking. Knock and keep on knocking. Seek and keep on seeking."

We would never think of looking for gold nuggets in our living rooms. We would never try to catch a big wave in our back yards. We would never entertain the idea of fishing for salmon in our bathrooms. As silly as these illustrations sound, they reveal that we know what it is to go wherever we need to go to find what we are looking for. God expects the same of us. Oftentimes, not a noble action is required, just movement that reveals true hunger for more. Faith is revealed by actions.

Jesus gave the disciples authority to drive out demons (see Mark 3:14–15), yet they were unable to bring deliverance to the boy whose story is told in Mark 9. Jesus explained that fasting and prayer were necessary. If the disciples already had sufficient power and authority, what would fasting and prayer do?

It was for their sakes. Fervent prayer, fasting and sustained pursuit of God's purposes work to shape us. They change us. These expressions of hunger transform us into vessels that can contain what God is releasing to us. Without those transformational experiences, we are prone to lose the very things God releases to us.

Refined character is the result, creating a place for God to release the weightiness of His work on the earth. It is His glory. Without refined character that can only be formed through perseverance, we will quickly lose the very gift of God given to us. Proverbs 20:21 warns us that an inheritance gained too quickly will not be blessed in the end. God is the ultimate giver of inheritance. And while He gives it to us all at once through promise, only faith can make the withdrawals. What is in my possession is different from what is in my account.

Prayer

Papa God, I never want to assume that all the actions in life are up to You. I am willing to go anywhere, and do anything to live in all that You have promised. Help me to live simply and humbly, always willing to do anything necessary to go to the next level. I am hungry for more. And I want the "more" You pour into my life to bring glory to the name of Jesus forever!

Confession

Jesus has already given me everything needed to make me successful now and throughout eternity. This He did at Calvary. I have set my heart to live by faith, making the withdrawals necessary to bring Him glory by pursuing all He has for me in this life.

62

Hope

If those who do not walk with God can do miracles, then those who walk with God are without excuse.

The great debate over whether or not God still does miracles in our midst rages on in many religious camps. We can be thankful that the anti-miracle camp is shrinking in numbers, as God's power is being made manifest increasingly all over the world. Tragically, though, doubt still affects many lives. It is the new believers I am most concerned about. They grow up hearing lies and in turn reject their purpose for being. They miss out on the hope of their calling that is meant to keep them alive and prospering, regardless of the season they are in.

Since the Bible does not remotely teach this concept—that Jesus is the same yesterday, today and forever, except for when He changed—anti-miracle proponents have to twist Scripture to have it say what they want. The verses I hear most often applied this way are Matthew 7:21–23:

> "Not everyone who says to Me, 'Lord, Lord,' will enter the kingdom of heaven, but he who does the will of My Father who

is in heaven will enter. Many will say to me on that day, 'Lord, Lord, did we not prophesy in Your name, and in Your name cast out demons, and in Your name perform many miracles?' And then I will declare to them, 'I never knew you; Depart from me, you who practice lawlessness.'"

The implication of the naysayers is that when we testify to miracles we have seen Jesus do, we are among those who will not enter the Kingdom, because this verse was aimed at us, and people like us.

Let's take a closer look at what Jesus actually taught in this passage. He identified three vital things in this discourse, addressing two groups of people. The first group is those who do not enter heaven simply by virtue of calling Him Lord. If what we call Him is not backed up in our lives by doing His will, then our confessions of Him as Lord are meaningless. What is His will? It is *on earth as it is in heaven.* Jesus Christ illustrated it perfectly, as He came to do the Father's will (see John 6:38). When the man with leprosy wanted to be healed, he told Jesus that if He was willing, He could heal him. Jesus said He was willing. It was His will (see Matthew 8:2–3). Over and over again the Bible says He healed and/or delivered *all.* You can never go wrong by doing what Jesus did.

The second group of people He addressed did what the first group missed. They did His will—they prophesied, cast out devils and performed miracles. But they did these things without two greater priorities functioning in their lives. The first thing missing for them was intimacy with God; He said He never knew them. God can know all about us, but can know us with intimate knowledge only to the degree that we open ourselves to Him. That is why confession is the beginning of our relationship with God. It is the act of opening ourselves to Him. Secondly, this group of people also practiced lawlessness. Their lives were inconsistent with the purpose of the miracles they were performing. Miracles are signs that bring people to Jesus, and that leads to freedom. Lawlessness is the opposite of freedom. For that reason, these two groups of people must depart from Him.

You cannot have false prophets unless you have real ones. You cannot have false signs and wonders unless there are real ones to compare them to. The counterfeit would be nonexistent if the real did not exist first. It is silly at best for people who do not have signs and wonders to argue against them. All fire is strange fire to those without fire. If those who live lawlessly perform miracles, then those who claim to be right with God must do them all the more! There is simply *no excuse*.

The most revelatory prayer prayed by anyone other than Jesus has to be the prayer of Ephesians 1:18–23. Here is a small part of it: "I pray that the eyes of your heart may be enlightened, so that you will know what is the hope of His calling. . . . He put all things in subjection under His feet, and gave Him as head over all things to the church, which is His body, the fullness of Him who fills all in all." Our hope is connected to the fact that all powers have been placed under His feet, and we, the Church, are His Body. The demonstration of His power, through people who have become open and honest before Him, turning from a life of lawlessness, is essential for an adequate witness of Jesus on the earth.

And this, true followers of Jesus, is our call.

Prayer

Dear heavenly Father, the fact that You are the One who called me to life is a hope beyond all dreams and desires. But now that You have called me, I want to please You with demonstrating Your will. I want to know Your heartbeat for people and live with the awareness that nothing is impossible with You. I commit myself to demonstrate Your will, according to the grace working in me, all for the glory of God.

Confession

I was created to be able to demonstrate the will of God. It is in my God-given DNA to hunger and long for His will to be demonstrated all around me. I will not settle for anything less. And by His grace, I will manifest these things that He might be glorified, and that people might be free.

63

Love

A bitter reaction to the sins of others is often worse than the sins of others.

That statement makes very little sense at first glance. So many atrocities have been done throughout history. It is hard to imagine a bitter reaction to evil actually being worse than the original act. In that way, my statement is wrong. But look at it this way: Jesus, who is perfect, taught us that those who want to be forgiven must forgive.

The most compelling parable that Jesus told along this line was about a man who had been forgiven of an astonishing debt of millions of dollars, but who then refused to forgive the debt of someone who owed him something like twenty dollars. The one who originally forgave the man with the massive debt rescinded that decision and instead had him imprisoned for refusing to forgive his neighbor's small debt. The point is rather clear: If you want to be forgiven, you must forgive. Jesus also taught that those who are forgiven must forgive as well.

All of my sins were against a perfect God. The only one who Himself is pure, the only one who has the absolute right not to forgive, chose to forgive me. The least sin committed against One who is perfect is far greater than the greatest sin committed against another sinner. That is the point of Jesus' parable. We who have been forgiven such horrible sins committed against a holy and perfect God must demonstrate that same forgiveness by how we treat others. It is a must.

When a sin is committed against us, it has a devastating effect on our lives. What is the one thing that could make it worse? Not forgiving the one who sinned against us. Perhaps you have heard the statement that goes something like this: "Not to forgive because you hope the other person will suffer is like drinking poison hoping someone else will die." That is the nature of bitterness and unforgiveness. It kills its owner.

One of the most sobering statements in the Bible about this subject is found in Hebrews 12:15: "See to it that no one comes short of the grace of God; that no root of bitterness springing up causes trouble, and by it many be defiled." This is one sin that has the power to contaminate and infect many others. The implication is that innocent people are defiled. Elsewhere, Jesus talked about being a stumbling block to others, that it would be better to have a millstone tied around one's neck and be cast into the sea (see Mark 9:42). Bitterness defiles, causing collateral damage.

My unforgiveness puts me in the same category of sin that I despise. At that moment, I become most like the person I have judgment against. This kind of heart blinds us to our own heart conditions, or we would never allow such a defilement to enter our lives. In forgiveness, I lay down my right to condemn, giving to the other the same mercy I want God to give to me. Forgiving others is an investment into my own future, for the merciful will obtain mercy (see Matthew 5:7).

Love forgives because love invests in people's freedom often before they want it or even know they need it or that it is possible. I call it an investment because of the likelihood of a return—people being set free. People who are forgiven long before they want it or even know they need it are much more likely to be drawn into a discovery of God's forgiveness. This is the beauty of life: to be able to bring others into God's forgiveness.

Prayer

Dear heavenly Father, thank You for forgiving me. I know there is nothing I could ever do to earn such a priceless gift from You. Help me to stay free from bitterness by being quick to forgive. And help me never to forget how privileged I am to give the gift You have given me to others, that You might be glorified.

Confession

I am forgiven by God. I did not earn forgiveness, but I can and will give it away. As a representative of His Kingdom, I will freely give the gift of forgiveness that was given to me. I set my heart to forgive quickly and lay down my right to demand the judgment of others. I purpose to live this way that God might be glorified through me.

64

Faith

The playing field of our faith is as big as our recognition of God's goodness.

Faith explores the realms opened by the promises of God found in the Person of Jesus Christ. These promises contain some of the greatest revelations ever received by mankind. They reveal the nature and heart of God. This is the most unexplored territory in existence. It is eternally great and far more vast than one could comprehend in a lifetime of exploration. This is the next great adventure. And it will last throughout all eternity.

Those who never make the connection with God's goodness struggle constantly with the expectation of tragedy. This fight creates unnecessary conflict any time they try to discern the source of a problem. Many attribute the clear work of the devil to God Himself because, as we have seen, they truly believe that God authors bad things to happen for our good. In other words, *the end justifies the means.* We would not accept this standard of logic in any other area of life. Yet it has become common in the theology of many, simply because they do not understand the cornerstone of all theology—God is really good. I would be arrested for child abuse if I did to my children what many say God does to His; this shows there is a good chance deception is involved here. This is not as complicated as many make it out to be. Goodness in heaven is at least as good as goodness here on earth.

When the issue of God's goodness is settled, our assignment becomes much clearer. There are many ways to illustrate this truth. When a person begins to burn with the conviction that God is good, things begin to open in her understanding that were closed before. Realms of possibilities present themselves in a way that requires exploration. And that is the pleasure and joy of faith—to explore the world of possibilities made available through God's goodness. Instead of living in reaction to problems, hoping for breakthroughs and solutions, we live proactively, looking for occasions for God's love and goodness to be manifest.

I watch daily as our church family looks for problems to address in His name. And it is really amazing to see what happens when believers take that approach rather than one of a defensive posture, protecting what I have in God. Remember Jesus' story of the man given the one talent (an amount of money) to invest (see Matthew 25:24–26)? Protecting what he had was the worst possible option. This is a Kingdom of advancement, and requires forward movement. My claim is this: We move forward in faith, according to our understanding and conviction of God's perfect goodness.

This brings us to the challenge of the hour—is it possible to live in pursuit of God's manifested goodness in places that have never seen it? Is it possible to look for problems, knowing that God's purpose is in the deliverance, not the affliction? Is it possible to activate our faith in His goodness enough to give us an appetite to see these things changed that have raised their arrogant heads against the knowledge of Jesus Christ?

My answer is yes to all of these issues. This is our time to get the goodness issue settled. And then out of that conviction, we can look for chances to let our faith explore the boundaries of goodness that are much more extreme than we could possibly imagine.

Prayer

Father, I long to be one who burns with the conviction of Your unquestionable goodness. I am tired of doubting or tainting one of the most basic foundations of all Scripture: Your goodness. Heal my own heart as it pertains to this truth. I want to be a part of the body of people that You entrust with all that is necessary to display Your nature to the world. It longs for this. And I want to make sure the world sees who You really are: a perfect Father, who is intensely good beyond measure.

Confession

I confess with my mouth and believe with my heart that God is perfectly good, all the time. No evil or darkness exists in Him. There are no hidden agendas where God really takes pleasure in the punishment or suffering of mankind. I, therefore, embrace the call to display the goodness of God daily, and look for problems to address in His name, that He might be glorified.

65

Hope

Worshipers are positioned by God to summon nations to their destinies.

The Psalms are songs of worship. The nature of the worship expression as prescribed by David is found on both sides of the cross. It is affirmed in the first Jerusalem council in Acts 15, and shapes more than our music. It defines our nature as believers—we are worshipers first.

The Psalms are more than a complement to the theological books of Scripture: They are filled with more revelation than I think we usually give them credit for. These are songs written *in* the glory of God. Insights exist in here that we cannot find anywhere else in Scripture, giving hope for things we might otherwise lose sight of. God's view of nations is one of those great surprises found in the Psalms. And while there are many judgmental statements made in this book that are certainly fitting for the day they were written in, there are also many songs with New Covenant themes, sung prophetically about a coming day—our day. These songs we must hold dear as ones that can shape the course of world history.

Here are a few that carry Jesus' heart for nations:

"All the ends of the earth will remember and turn to the LORD, and all the families of the nations will worship before You"

(Psalm 22:27). This one has extreme importance for us because Psalm 22 is one of the most important Messianic psalms. Many details of Jesus' crucifixion are found here. It seems only right to watch Jesus get the reward for His suffering—nations, made up of surrendered families found in worship.

"Let the nations be glad and sing for joy; for You will judge the peoples with uprightness and guide the nations on the earth" (Psalm 67:4). The context for this verse is salvation visiting the nations. This joy is found in their salvation and gives them guidance into His purposes. But the revelation of this great event was given to those who knew God as a loving Father, desiring to bless His children (see Psalm 67:1–3).

"All nations whom You have made shall come and worship before You, O Lord, and they shall glorify Your name" (Psalm 86:9). Nations will find the purpose for their creation. Their design is revealed in their salvation, and then they come full circle and worship. This insight was given to those in the glory, before the New Covenant was ever established.

"So the nations will fear the name of the LORD and all the kings of the earth Your glory" (Psalm 102:15). Nations, along with their leaders, will come to a proper fear of God before all of this is over. That fear is the beginning of wisdom, and wisdom is reformational in its effect. This picture of reformation was given to those who were in the glory, ministering to God.

"I will give thanks to You, O LORD, among the peoples, and I will sing praises to You among the nations" (Psalm 108:3). This is a wonderful description of the peoples of the world giving a healthy expression of praise and honor to God. In this case, the nations are made up of people who surrender to their loving God.

"Praise the LORD, all nations; laud Him, all peoples!" (Psalm 117:1). This verse illustrates my beginning statement quite clearly. It is the picture of worshipers summoning nations to God.

These songs literally came out of the glory of God. That place of presence, that place of undefiled worship, was the womb of revelation of God's heart for the nations. It is in that presence that we find out what our responsibility is—to sing and declare the destinies and purposes of God for the nations.

As important as sound theology is, the purpose behind singing and declaring these songs of destiny goes far beyond being biblically correct. It is the act of summoning nations to their reason for being, and doing so out of the throne room of the almighty God. This is the privilege and responsibility of worshipers. From the glory, and a heart filled with great hope, we declare over the nations what the Father is saying.

Prayer

Heavenly Father, thank You for giving us the great honor of worshiping You with clean hearts. You made that possible. And thank You for letting us feel your heart in the process. I desire to say what You are saying and summon the nations to their purposes and destinies. Help me to do this effectively, all for Your glory.

Confession

I embrace the privilege of carrying God's heart for the nations, for all peoples of the world. And by God's grace operating in me, I will declare His heart for the nations of the world, that the Lamb of God will receive the reward of His sufferings. I do these things for the glory of God.

66

Love

It is impossible to reach our
potential without learning
to minister to ourselves.

One of the most important lessons for us to learn in life is
how to minister to ourselves. It is vital. It is so important
that God will blind the eyes and deafen the ears of our closest
friends so that we might be positioned to discover what He has
already taught us that we have lost sight of. It is not punishment
but rather His kindness leading us to our God-given strength.
Often this kind of love positions us for our greatest promotion.

Knowing how to minister to ourselves has its anchor in what
God says about us. Ministry to ourselves draws from God's heart
of love and applies directly to ours. It is using God's Word to
bring strength, understanding or just plain faith where we feel
weak or confused.

Biblical meditation seems to be a lost art in many parts of the
Church. Perhaps there is fear of it because of its counterfeit—
Eastern meditation. The cultic version, which directs people to
empty their minds, opens them to outside influence—and more
times than not it is demonic. In biblical meditation, we fill our
minds with what God is saying. In that process, we run it over

and over in our hearts and minds until understanding increases from the inside out. It may seem strange to say, but oftentimes our hearts get it before our minds do. My heart can burst with excitement over a truth that I cannot as yet fully articulate. That is okay. The process has begun. It is a divine process. It should not surprise us to discover that our spirits perceive truth before our minds.

There is something profoundly healing and refreshing that comes only from the presence of the Lord. Thanksgiving and praise help us enter that place. Something happens to the heart when we choose to honor Him in spite of our loss, trouble or place of weakness. Giving Him praise turns our attention from ourselves to Him. That is never a bad idea. Where this has really brought strength into my life is when I give Him praise for the very things I might question because of the problems I am facing. When facing the threat of disease, for example, I exalt Him as the healer. Please notice that this must not be a token expression. In fact, I have noticed that the darker the cloud over me, the more demonstrative I must become in expressing my heart for Him.

It is called a sacrifice, which is a step beyond convenience. At this point, rejoicing is the last thing I want to do in the natural. But I refuse to live confined by the natural. I choose, therefore, to move into a superior realm called the realm of faith. From that place, I rejoice and rejoice and rejoice. When we were in the world, we knew that joy preceded rejoicing. But in the Kingdom, rejoicing often precedes joy.

The last part of my *strengthening myself* process is seen in the company I choose to keep. I intentionally associate with people of great faith, hope and love. Some people drain you. When you are the most vulnerable in your faith is when you must become the most focused on whom you will allow to affect you. This is called wisdom, and wisdom is necessary, especially when our spiritual immune system is weakened. While it might not seem as though I am ministering to myself in this situation, I am, in fact, choosing the environment I have purposed to live in. This is part of the equation for health.

While there might be some who take this as an invitation to independence and rebellion, those things only exacerbate the real problem. God describes us as members of one another, members of His Body on earth. The picture is beautiful and beyond comprehension. I resist any teaching that tends to lead people into independence and rebellion. Separation from the Body has caused many to be defiled.

David is my hero in this regard. He went through a series of rejections: from Saul, to his brethren, to the Philistines he had served, to the mighty men whose lives he saved from self-destruction. Each of these seasons seemed to lead further and further away from God's purpose for his life—to become king of Israel. Little did he know that what seemed to take him far from the throne was actually taking him to the back door of the throne room. But the key that unlocked the door was strengthening himself in the Lord (see 1 Samuel 30:6). Learning to minister to himself was the final lesson that took him to his divine potential—being the king of Israel.

Prayer

Dear heavenly Father, I do not want to live overwhelmed by what I do not understand or have control of. Instead, I want to see through Your eyes. You see me differently than I do, and I am the one who needs to change. So please help me to see what You say about me in a way that increases my dependence and delight in You. I ask this for Your glory.

Confession

God's strength is my portion and a part of my inheritance, for He is my strength. I will display His strength that He will receive honor by my stepping into His purposes for my life. And may the grace of God upon my life bring Him glory forever.

67

Faith

Faith explores what revelation reveals.

Imagine receiving a great inheritance of thousands of acres of land. Picture yourself standing on a hill and having the attorney point to a ridge off in the distance, saying, "You own everything between here and there." Then imagine him pointing in another direction and announcing that you own all the land between here and that river. And so his descriptions go, pointing to things in the landscape that mark the boundaries of your inheritance. He announces it is all yours. That would certainly be great news. I cannot speak for you, but I would want to explore every bit of land I just inherited. To look at it from a distance and be satisfied with ownership would be an insult to those who paid a great price to leave something for me to enjoy.

So it is in the Kingdom. What Jesus gave us, that which cost Him everything, must be explored thoroughly. And faith is the vehicle that takes us on that great adventure.

So many believers spend their lives standing on that hill, confessing what is theirs, but never actually experiencing it firsthand. The pronouncement of ownership even takes on the element of pride with confession after confession, as they proclaim their great authority and purpose. It is okay for that to be a starting place, but it is a great tragedy when we stay there. What God provided for us was not meant to be reduced to a confession. Instead, it was meant to be the invitation to pursue, apprehend and enjoy! It is the invitation to an adventure, the ultimate journey—for all that belongs to Jesus is ours to enjoy. It is unlimited in scope and can never be completely explored in this life. But that is no excuse to remain idle. This Kingdom must be enjoyed.

This is where my life in the secret place pays off most. It is there, alone with God, that I have the responsibility and privilege to be intensely specific in my requests. If I keep running into people going bankrupt, there is my assignment. If it seems as though everyone with sugar diabetes crosses my path, there is my assignment. If it seems as though marriages are crumbling around me, I must cry out for the insight and anointing needed to help bring about victory in those situations.

The Lord often uses the needs of people around me to alert me to what is available for me to pursue on their behalf. I do not believe the Lord simply wants me to carry their burdens. While showing compassion and mercy is vital, so is obtaining answers. Jesus was not known for comforting people in their problems and then leaving them to figure things out on their own. Within the King's domain—the Kingdom—is the answer for every problem humanity will ever face. And those who "seek first His Kingdom" are those who are entrusted with the answers needed to change the circumstances and transform the people.

This is the beautiful privilege of those who discover the vastness of this inheritance. We must let faith take us into places in God we could never enter otherwise.

Prayer

Father, I am wonderfully overwhelmed by all that You have given to me in Jesus Christ. It is beyond my ability to comprehend. And even though my inheritance is so vast, I pray for the gift of holy dissatisfaction with the status quo. I do not want to be satisfied with theories instead of tasting the realities of Your world that could change my life, as well as the lives of others, for all eternity. Please open my eyes to see what You have given me to pursue, what You have given me to apprehend, what You have given me to enjoy. My cry is that Your name will be exalted, and that people will become free through everything I taste of. You are truly good, always good. Thanks.

Confession

I refuse to be satisfied with theories and classroom ideals. I must taste and see that the Lord is good. My inheritance is vast and is beyond all comprehension. But it is not beyond my ability to taste and see. I commit myself, therefore, to a life of exploration, that God might be glorified and that people might see Jesus in me.

68

Hope

When God says no, a better yes is coming.

A person who lives with an abiding understanding of God's abundant goodness interprets the day-to-day stuff much differently than everyone else. Prayer is one of those necessary elements of the believer's life that is sometimes as painful as it is rewarding. I can honestly admit that it is the lifestyle of prayer that has brought some of my greatest joys, which are then contrasted with some of my greatest frustrations.

Part of that frustrating journey is learning what to do with a *no* from God. And sometimes what is even worse is *silence* from God. For me it is more painful than no. I have learned to take comfort in the Psalms, as the psalmist often mentioned his frustration with God's silence. Both the no and the silence are something we have been given to steward. It is an extremely important part of the process called maturity. It would be incorrect to say or imply that God is ignoring me or is unconcerned. Even if I feel that way, I must return to truth and embrace the fact that He is a perfect, loving father, who excels beyond my wildest dreams at being my Father—Papa God. He cares more than I do about any circumstance or dream I may have. He is that good.

Oftentimes silence from God means He has already given me the direction, insight or capacity for the situation. You have heard the phrase that someone is giving you "the silent treatment." It is that person's form of punishment. God's silence is never punishment. Only in silence will I find what He has already downloaded into my heart. In that place, things come to the surface that I would not have been able to hear otherwise. It is as though the deep of God calls to the deep in me, bringing to the surface what might otherwise be untapped. It is painful, but needed.

I find the no of God fascinating, especially when you contrast it with what Jesus stated over and over again to His disciples: that they could have anything they asked for. It is interesting, though, that when James and John asked for the right to call down fire on the Samaritans, Jesus rebuked them and said no (see Luke 9:54–56). No is God's trump card, used when a better yes is coming, or when a yes would undermine His eternal purposes.

One of the great stories in this regard is in John 11. Lazarus is sick and dying. Mary and Martha send a notice to Jesus saying, "He whom You love is sick" (verse 3). In other words, someone You already have a relationship with needs help, which should trump Your obligation to minister to the strangers You are presently with. Jesus states that the sickness is not unto death, and then stays where He is two more days (verses 4–6). Emphasis is put on Jesus' love for this family, and then it states that He stays two more days without going to attend to their requests. Very few of us would interpret staying away from someone's crisis moment as love. But that is what the God of love did.

If Jesus had gone immediately to minister to Lazarus, there certainly would have been a healing. Because He waited, there was a resurrection. No one day, became a bigger yes on another.

Living with hope that finds its anchor in the nature and promises of God enables us to discover the richness of God as a Father and stay away from panic. In stewarding our hearts well, we learn to live knowing things will turn out even better than if we had had our own way.

Prayer

Dear heavenly Father, thank You for Your goodness that surpasses all comprehension. I rest in hope in the knowledge that You are looking out for me, with the loving heart of a Father. Help me with my tendency to panic when things do not work the way I think they should, and especially help and forgive me for the times I have thought You did not care. I know that is not possible. Please give me the grace never to go there again. I pray these things for Your honor and glory.

Confession

God is always good. He is a perfect, loving Father with my best always in mind. Instead of accusing Him of not caring, I will quiet my heart to find His purposes in my more confusing circumstances. I declare that I love the will of God and will yield to His purposes, all for His glory.

69

Love

Evangelism in its purest form
is an overflow of worship.

These two subjects are intricately woven together in the heart, much more than we might think at first glance. The one difference is the level of urgency: worship, while absolutely appropriate and necessary now, will continue throughout eternity, while evangelism is only for this lifetime.

That might move some into thinking that evangelism is the believer's top priority. After all, the saving of souls is paramount while we are still on this planet. That is, until you see that loving God first, along with all of its expressions and nuances, is actually what adds definition, power and presence to our evangelistic efforts.

There is a powerful connection between our love for God and our love for people. Evangelism often gets reduced to people becoming projects, and people hate being someone else's project. Who wants to be the project of some religious zealot so he can feel good about his devotion to God? No one wants to be the notch on the back of someone's Bible. Perhaps this is part of the reason that evangelism gets such a bad rap.

Yet evangelism is real and necessary, a passionate delight of our Father. He wants all to be brought into His family. An overriding theme of the New Testament message through Jesus Christ was that we are to love one another. *Another* for Jesus was more than just members of our families or even our church families. For Jesus, it was the man who was robbed and left for dead until the good Samaritan rescued him. For Jesus, it was the tax man who climbed the tree to see Him better, or the woman caught in the act of adultery. For Jesus, *another* was Pilate, who refused to release Him, the thief who hung next to Him on a cross, and the religious leaders who worked against His purposes. *Another* represents the people for whom He would die.

There can be no greater love in our hearts than our love for God. Anything we love above Him is idolatry. Yet our love for God, displayed through passionate worship, adds fuel and definition to our love for people. The second is enhanced by the first.

I remember a conversation with a young man from Sweden who loved his girlfriend very much. He was afraid to surrender to Christ because he thought it would take away from his ability to love her. Besides the obvious issue of putting her before God, he was missing the wonderful reality of how loving God first would affect the rest of his life. For me, I am actually capable of loving my wife more than I would be if she were number one. That is another one of those apparent contradictions of living in God's Kingdom. In the same way that we live by dying, or that we are exalted by humbling ourselves, so I love my wife more by loving God first.

This concept is also true as it pertains to evangelism. Loving God first, best and most passionately releases us to love people more authentically and more effectively. Evangelism then becomes fueled by our love for God.

When Isaiah saw the Lord high and lifted up (see Isaiah 6), we read about the overwhelming sense of God's presence one would expect. But the part that moves me most is Isaiah's response.

God asked, "Whom shall I send?"

Isaiah said, "Send me!"

Anyone who truly worships God sees God's heart. And anyone who truly sees God's heart will have a similar response to that of this great prophet. "Send me!" This means that evangelism, being sent by God into the harvest fields, is never better than when it comes from the heart of the worshiper who has actually seen the heart of God in worship.

Prayer

My Father and my God, I love You. I love to worship You and give You honor. You are worthy of all glory, honor and praise. This is my delight. My passion is to touch Your heart in a way that glorifies You. But please help me never to become complacent in my affections for You at the expense of those who have not yet been brought in the family. Strengthen my zeal for worship in a way that affects my passion for the lost. I pray these things that the name of Jesus might be held in highest honor.

Confession

I was born to worship. Everything about me is an expression of God's design enabling me to worship well. He has equipped me to serve and minister to Him effectively. I embrace this as a privileged lifestyle that God might be glorified, both in my worship, and through the people who are drawn to Him through my love.

70

Faith

No one was ever criticized, scolded or corrected by Jesus for seeking His gifts.

It has become common for people to talk about seeking God's face instead of His hand. I understand the idea behind it, as a relationship with God is much more important than a physical miracle. But you just cannot find such reasoning in any of the conversations with Jesus recorded in Scripture. In this metaphor, God's face represents a relationship; His hand represents what He can give us. But for me, that is really too much information. I tell people that if they have been seeking His hand and not His face, just look up. They are not that far apart. One leads to the other, according to Jesus.

Sometimes people without experience give the weirdest counsel to those who need a miracle. In the absence of power is a lot of foolish religious reasoning. The blind beggar Bartimaeus cried out for Jesus, saying, "Jesus, Son of David, have mercy on me!" (Mark 10:47). He was seeking healing. Jesus did not scold him and say it was more important that he get to know the Healer. Of course, that is true, but that is not the approach that Jesus took when ministering to Bartimaeus, or anyone else for that matter. So why do we? Probably because all too often Bartimaeus' eyes are still blind after we have prayed for him.

A couple very dear to me just found out this week that their newborn baby is completely deaf. That is devastating news for them and for us. Of course, someone thought they would try to help them with their challenge and point out the fact that being deaf is such a blessing. The deaf get to develop other parts of their lives to make up for what they are missing by not hearing. Even if that is true, it is stupid reasoning. You can only come up with ideas like that in the absence of miracles. Jesus has given the example to follow—the authority to be commissioned with access to the same power from on high. In some ways, the rest is up to us.

Jesus took a different approach: "If I do them [the works of the Father, the miracles], though you do not believe Me, believe the works, so that you may know and understand that the Father is in Me, and I in the Father" (John 10:38). Jesus was okay with their not believing in Him (which sounds very strange to say), if they believed the works He did. In believing the works, the miracles, they would know the Father was in Him and He in the Father.

That is a stunning realization. Jesus came to reveal the Father, which cannot adequately be done apart from miracles. And He was even okay with people wondering about Him, as long as they did not wonder about the miracles. The miracles revealed the Father. As a result of this realization, they would naturally believe in Jesus.

In other words, what came from His hand took them to His face.

Prayer

Heavenly Father, please help me to stay away from all excuses or reasoning that could insulate people from the courage to cry out to

You. Clothe me with power from on high again and again and again. Please help me to reveal the Father through a life of miracles, and to bring practical solutions to people's lives just as any good father would do. Help me to live this way, for the glory of God.

Confession

Jesus accomplished everything necessary for me to follow in His footsteps. And even though my efforts do not equal His, I refuse to lower the expectations for my life to an acceptable norm. I embrace the privilege of revealing the Father through miracles, signs and wonders. I do these things for the glory of God.

71

Hope

God wants our minds to be renewed so that our will can be done.

I realize that this statement seems to be off a bit, but, honestly, consider it. I am more convinced than ever that this is the heart of God for each of us.

This is not a bid for our rights as believers. It is not a new teaching on "How to get your own way with God." Quite the opposite! The almighty One transforms us that we might transform everything around us. We all know that the last thing we need is more self-willed Christians fighting for what they want and think they deserve. A self-centered Gospel is not the Gospel at all, as it is not the Good News it claims to be.

We also know by now that God was not interested in creating robots that would automatically do anything He programmed them to do. That would have been easy. Deliberate partnership is of supreme value to God. This is especially true when we consider that humanity is the only part of creation that was created like God—in His image. Our purpose for being is wrapped up in the concept of co-laboring with Him, helping to turn the nature of our world into a mirrored image of His.

When God saved us, He restored us to His purpose of co-laboring and co-reigning. I do not think it has really hit us yet, but the hope of our calling is connected to our being in Christ, and—purely from that place of presence—having authority over every name and power that has ever existed. This is what Paul prayed we would understand. Look again at these verses:

> I pray that the eyes of your heart may be enlightened, so that you will know what is the hope of His calling . . . and what is the surpassing greatness of His power toward us who believe. These are in accordance with the working of the strength of His might which He brought about in Christ. . . . And He put all things in subjection under His feet.
>
> Ephesians 1:18-20

As you can imagine, if we really get that part of the equation about hope, we will worry a lot less about the rest.

This entire life of ours is about learning how to reign. The purpose of prayer is to learn how to reign. The purpose behind our life of discipline and devotion is to learn how to reign. The reason behind our need for divine order in our lives as it pertains to family, business, health and overall well-being is that we are learning to reign. The apostle Paul described this, saying that we "will reign in life through the One, Jesus Christ" (Romans 5:17). The Passion Translation of Proverbs captures this thought of "reigning in life" quite well, page after page. It thrills me! No one who truly sees this plan of God could become haughty or arrogant. I do not think it is possible. There is an overwhelming sense of undeserved favor on this one that endears us to God in worship. It is a privilege of the highest order.

Jesus is the One who set the grounds rules. He turned to His disciples and offered them the deal of a lifetime. Remember: He said numerous times that they could have anything they asked for. It is not as though this promise was without conditions. In one of the promises, for example, He said, "If you abide in Me, and My words abide in you, ask whatever you wish, and it will be done for you" (John 15:7). Jesus then went on to say that this process is one of the ways the Father is glorified. Think of it—the Father is glorified by His plan working, which is you getting what you have asked for. This is amazing! Whenever we get an answer to our prayers, it is a testimony that God's plan of co-laboring and co-reigning actually works.

Perhaps this is part of what is implied in Ephesians 3:10: "So that the manifold wisdom of God might now be made known through the church to the rulers and the authorities in the heavenly places." For all of creation to know of God's greatness through Him is a no-brainer. God wants the heavenly realm to learn from the redeemed ones, who represent His heart well in all matters. This is the testimony of God's wisdom. His plan works.

It comes down to this: Our minds must be renewed so that we use this undeserved position of authority and responsibility in a way that brings Him glory. It must be consistent with His heart, His ideals and His purposes. He longs to see a generation who can ask for whatever they want, and have it completely fit into His plan for planet earth. And by this He is glorified.

Prayer

Heavenly Father, I need to think bigger. Your plans and purposes for my life are so much greater than I ever imagined. Please teach me what and how You think. I want to use my life well, that I might demonstrate Your wisdom to all the powers in heavenly places. These are the things I long for that You may be honored and glorified.

Confession

I will not allow the fact that I am in a position I could never earn to keep me from my God-given assignment. It is not about me; it is about Him. He must be glorified by all that exists because His plan of co-laboring with His people has proven to be wise. I will live unto this end, that God might receive glory forever and ever.

72

Love

False humility will keep us
from our destinies, but true
humility will take us to them.

False humility is often seen in self-abasement, self-criticism and self-condemnation. The word *self* in each of these phrases should give us a clue as to what kind of humility this is—it is counterfeit humility. It is the most dangerous form of pride because it is thought of as a spiritual value, which gives it permission to stay. As such, it is guarded and protected as though it were a godly trait.

Jesus taught us to love our neighbors as we love ourselves. This is a challenge for those embracing the selfless lifestyle of Jesus. It almost seems like a contradiction. But it is not. It is one of those apparent paradoxes of Scripture that are essential for our well-being. We stay healthy only as we embrace both sides of the issue simultaneously.

To love ourselves as Jesus described does not lead to self-centeredness or selfishness. It is what keeps us healthy and strong in the things of God. Jesus taught this as the second great commandment. Paul said that this role is one of *nourishing* and *cherishing* our flesh (see Ephesians 5:29). We do this instinctively in many ways if we stay emotionally healthy.

I am careful around people who are highly critical of themselves. Those who are easily moved to judge themselves harshly will probably do the same to me when the occasion arises, for we tend to love others the way we love ourselves. The Bible says, "Let another praise you, and not your own mouth" (Proverbs 27:2). Self-promotion is not a good way to live. Praising oneself is a disgusting practice, unless it is done by a three-year-old. Then it is cute. But maturity means we pull away from seeing the world rotating around us, and we take on the position of becoming what is best for the world. I think we get the meaning of that verse quite well, as most of us would not feel comfortable praising ourselves, even if it came to mind. We have too much social skill to do such a thing. But it is the first part of the verse that caught me off guard one day. *Let another praise you.* I will be honest. This is very uncomfortable for me. But this is a command. And it must be learned.

People give honor to an artist when they acknowledge the quality of a painting. The painting is an expression of the artist, and it receives the glory that belongs to the artist. The artist is not glorified by the painting criticizing itself, if that were possible. In a similar way, we are giving honor to God when we give honor to people. He takes it personally. This means that when someone gives me honor I have a responsibility before God. First of all, I give thanks to God for the privilege of being honored in His name. Secondly, I realize that all honor given to me is undeserved, in the sense that whatever is good did not originate with me. Thirdly, I must give that honor to Him, because He really is the One who deserves it. What I must not do is tell the person who is complimenting me, "Oh, it's not me; it's Jesus." Turning away their efforts to honor God by complimenting me is a dishonor to them, God and me. Honor—accept it, learn to enjoy it without taking credit for it and finally, give it to its rightful owner.

At some point we have to acknowledge God's work of grace in our lives for us to step into His purposes more fully. This confidence is frequently seen in the apostle Paul's life. And I doubt any of us would say he was arrogant or self-centered. His confidence in God's grace brought glory to God and stability to himself. As someone once said, *True humility is not thinking less of yourself; it is thinking of yourself less.* Our destinies await a people whose confidence in God's grace will take them where others fear to go.

Prayer

Heavenly Father, I know that everything good in my life is because of You. You are the source, and You are the reason. Thank You. Help me not to fall into the religiously acceptable practice of self-criticism. I know that ultimately it dishonors You. I simply want to glorify You in all I do and in all I am. I give You praise as the One who does all things well, even Your work in me. Thank You.

Confession

I refuse to protect self-criticism as a spiritual value, but instead will work to acknowledge His work of grace in me. If I am honored, I will give all the glory to God, as He is the author of all that is good in me. By God's grace, I will not deflect the honor given to me, but will instead show respect to the person giving the honor, again that God may be exalted. I do these things for the glory of God.

73

When we submit the things of
God to the mind of man, unbelief
and religion are the results. When
we submit the mind of man to the
things of God, miracles and the
renewed mind are the results.

At least a couple of times Scripture says that God sits in the heavens and laughs. Both times that I know of it is because He sees the plans the enemy has against His anointed and in opposition to His purposes. Apparently, it seems funny to God that finite beings think they can match wits with Him and effectively strategize against Him—a laughable concept for sure.

How true that it is that the fool says there is no God (see Psalm 14:1). And for some of the supposed greatest minds of the day to make such statements is entertaining to say the least. I find it interesting that people will spend their lives studying how the universe, the body or life is designed and come away thinking there is no designer. You cannot have a design without a designer.

The atheistic mindset influences the Church at times. I do not mean by this that believers conclude there is no God. We know better. I mean that people begin to respond to issues of life in the same way as their atheistic neighbors, without noticing that the thought processes are not that different. It should stand out to us. And while our theology does not allow for atheism, sometimes our lifestyles do. It is not okay to face life without having the God who invades the impossible at the center of our affections and pursuits. It is simply not okay—not for anyone who confesses Jesus as Lord.

I have noticed quite often that people need to be convinced that a real miracle has happened. X rays, doctors' reports, etc. are requested before they will believe. I understand that need, as there have been many fakes throughout history. The request for proof seems reasonable. But it should not be necessary—not for one who confesses Christ.

Don't get me wrong: The doctor's report that confirms a miracle is always an encouragement. We can welcome the medical community's confirmation of the works of God. But the fact that we need one to believe is not a sign of intellectual strength; it is a sign of weakness. It is an indicator that the thought *There is no God* is imbedded deep in our hearts. Instead of becoming people who pursue the breakthroughs that draw thousands or even millions into the Kingdom, we want evidence that He is what He says He is: the same yesterday, today and forever. He exists, but many think He is simply a force, without personality or concern or intent. Nothing could be further from the truth. He is God: Father God. He is a real father who loves people—really loves people.

Submitting the things of God to that mindset seldom works out well because we tend to require things of God we have no right to require. He has left us with enough evidence of His nature and heart to spur us on to change the world—literally. But whenever we submit our minds to what God is doing—wow!

Transformation takes place. It is beautiful to see a mind come under the influence of the work of the Holy Spirit. A transformation takes place that becomes the glorious example of His brilliance. While faith does not come from the mind, it is wonderful to see a mind illustrate and enhance the life of faith.

Prayer

Dear heavenly Father, please help me never to be intimidated by those whose intellectual strength is greater than mine. Please help me to see the full influence of my faith on how I think. I want to represent You well, illustrating how You think about how I live. I purpose to do these things for Your glory.

Confession

The renewed mind is my portion, my inheritance in Christ. I declare that it is the Father's good pleasure to teach me how He thinks, and in doing so, He will help me to remain childlike for His glory.

74

Hope

God disciplines us so His blessings will not kill us.

It is probably hard for most of us to imagine, but God really wants to bless us more than we want to be blessed. Pleasure, joy, love and beauty are things He has made. They are all His idea. And the role that these things have in our lives cannot be overestimated. They epitomize His nature and His world brilliantly. Blessings from God are small tastes of heaven on earth.

In the Kingdom, blessings equal responsibilities. But not in a punishing way. Rather, a blessing from God increases our awareness of His nature, and increases our capacity to delight in Him.

What does it mean when He said to pray for His will to be done here on earth as it is in heaven? Does that mean certain things that exist here are not supposed to? I think so. And we have the authority and responsibility to get rid of them. Disease does not exist in heaven, and, therefore, should not exist here. So what happens if everyone I pray for who has cancer is healed? What will happen to me? Would that be considered a blessing? First of all, I would become a household name all over the world within about thirty days. Private jets would land at our local airport daily with people carrying large amounts of money to try to persuade me to come and pray for their loved ones, who are too sick to travel.

Let's say that I could not be bought, and no amount of money could deter me from what God has called me to do. I still have a problem: Whenever I do pray for someone, I have the realization that for every yes there are a thousand nos. The media would no doubt give me a season of grace, boasting in the wonderful things that were being done. But in a very short time, they would look for dirt in my life, going through my trash to find a bounced check or perhaps an angry letter from a parishioner, or maybe talking to people I went to high school with to stir things up. We have noted that controversy sells papers and TV time, and many in those industries will create it if they have to.

And then there is the other temptation, one that most people probably think they would not have a problem with—the temptation to think I am something special. After all, people all over the world want an audience with me because of my cancer-healing gift. The pressure of facing that option day after day is way too much for many to handle.

So, do you think it would be God's will to give that kind of a gift to someone? I believe the answer is absolutely yes. Jesus did it. But were God to do that to me prematurely, the gift would crush me. In other words, the weightiness of such a responsibility would outweigh my ability to carry it faithfully for the glory of God. So the grace is available for us to do as Jesus did. And that would be the purpose for His discipline. With it, He makes sure my heart is refined enough to carry the weight of what I have asked for because blessings carry responsibilities. He disciplines us so we can survive His blessings.

Prayer

Dear heavenly Father, please help me to see Your kindness in all the times You discipline me by Your Word. I want to please You. And I desire to grow into rock-solid stability that can carry weighty things. I want You to be exalted for the gifts and blessings You gift to me. Help me to succeed at this for Your glory.

Confession

God's desire to bless me is greater than my desire to be blessed. Even in the times He corrects me, it is because of His passion to bless. So I position myself as a child of God who sincerely delights in my heavenly Father, that He might be glorified for all that He has done in me.

75

> Flattery is the counterfeit of
> honor. It is ultimately self-serving
> as it cheapens the privilege of
> recognizing greatness in another.

Giving honor to another person is one of the richest expressions of love we can give, both for the person and for God. If I see a beautiful building, I do not praise the building. I acknowledge its beauty, but credit the architect and builder. In the same way, giving honor is one of the ways we give glory to God. It is a great privilege for every believer to acknowledge the great work of God in other people. For it to be real, it cannot be dishonest, and it cannot be given hoping for something in return.

The apostle Paul teaches us that we are God's *workmanship* (see Ephesians 2:10). That word is where our word *poem* comes from. Whenever we give honor to people, we are reading a poem, the masterpiece of God, that He is writing in that person's life. It encourages them, it connects us to our assignment of being a strength to others and it brings glory to God. Honor is a beautiful thing.

Flattery, on the other hand, is dishonest in nature. It is careless and misleading, hoping for something in return. Sometimes those who want a culture of honor, but who do not have internal value for others, resort to this counterfeit in order to feel good about their lifestyles. It is empty and vain and does not accomplish what true honor can.

Honor requires a certain amount of discernment and prophetic gifting to be really effective. And by the way, both of those things are a part of the spiritual DNA of every believer. It is in us. And we are capable.

We are to give honor to people in several areas. First is for position and title. It is important for us to recognize that they have their positions because God raises up and casts down. It is foolish not to honor the one God honors. It is also true that sometimes the person's character is not up to his or her position. If, for example, a police officer tries to pull me over for breaking a law, yet I happen to know that he drinks too much, I cannot use that as an excuse to ignore him. I must pull over out of honor for the badge. Honor goes to the person and the position.

We give honor because of accomplishments. Sometimes it is because people obey God in a wonderful way, or they operate in their gifting with excellence, or do something that they really struggled to do that we applaud them. It is a beautiful part of life. I believe that God delights in such moments, as He is the One who made such accomplishments possible. He is the Father who takes pleasure in all that His children are able to do.

I love the verse that says, "The horse is prepared for the day of battle, but the victory belongs to the LORD" (Proverbs 21:31). This ties our efforts to the Lord's accomplishments and lets us in on a secret—God is involved in our victories; therefore, at the end of the day, we give Him all the glory.

We have the privilege of recognizing what God is doing deep inside a person. This honor is given for *who* a person is. It is his or her *being*. This is not seen through a casual glance. No, instead, this is something discerned only by those who are positioned to celebrate what God is doing.

One of the most important *poem readings* of my life came from a dear friend who talked with me about the things that he saw God forming in me, *embryonically*. He read the *poetry* in me that I could not read for myself. In other words, these things were alive, but were yet not evident through title or achievements. Because they were unseen, there was little temptation for me to go out and make this word happen. Instead, I chose to let faith and hope be the womb for this word given to me in love. Today I am living in what was described in that word given to me about thirty years ago.

Prayer

My Father and my God, I give You praise for all that You have done and are doing in me. Please increase my ability to see what You are doing in others so I can honor You by celebrating them. I want to read the masterpiece, the poetry You are writing in their lives so they will be encouraged and strengthened and You will be exalted for Your great work. I ask this for Your glory!

Confession

I will give honor to others sacrificially. I will do this because it is within my ability as a follower of Jesus Christ. It will not be for my benefit. It will be for the honor, strength and encouragement of others, and it will be for the glory of God.

76

Faith

Non-sacrificial people are of no consequence to the devil.

Jesus became poor that we might become rich. He gave everything so that our way into eternal life would be covered and paid for. There is nothing we can do to earn love, favor or salvation from God. It is a gift given freely to each of us because of the merit of Jesus Christ, the sacrificial lamb. Salvation is imparted to us simply because we believe that Jesus met the Father's demands due because of our sins.

No amount of sacrifice on my part, no effort to pay for my own sins, could ever qualify me as one capable of obtaining my own redemption from God. Only Jesus could pay such a price. Yet convenience and sacrifice cannot coexist. The *believing* believer is called to a higher level of life because we are favored.

"We love, because He first loved us" (1 John 4:19). Receiving His love equips us to do the same as He did. He set the standard for what love looks like. Our response is this: As He did for us, we do in return. Just as He gave His all for us, so we give our all for Him. But this is not an effort to earn any measure of our salvation. I give all to Him because I have favor. How could I respond any other way after receiving a gift I could never qualify for?

My heroes of the faith are many and are growing in number almost daily. There are several things about their lives that are unique to true world changers. Each of them is sacrificial, for instance, but none of them is impressed with his or her sacrifice. Paul taught us to present our bodies as living offerings. He then said this is our reasonable form of worship (see Romans 12:1). I find it interesting that in the Kingdom of God, the intellectual thing to do is to offer our bodies as an offering. Such a sacrifice is not to atone for sin; it is our offering because our sins are atoned for. It is the reasonable thing to do. The pressure to earn anything from God is about as far removed from the life of the believer as the east is from the west. It is a gift.

I often find people who think it is fine to live without sacrifice because of what Jesus accomplished for us. Their thought is that because Jesus did it, we have no need to. This is true, but only in part. I cannot earn forgiveness. But can I receive love and not love in return? Can I be favored of God and do nothing with that favor? The question we must ask is, What can I accomplish on His behalf now that I have permission to live as though I had never sinned?

What causes the powers of darkness to tremble the most is seeing a company of people who will pay any price, go to any lengths, to see God's purposes established on the earth. The power of the enemy's lies has no influence on those who no longer fear death. The fearless lifestyle of the sacrificial resets the standard of how this life can be lived for Jesus. It reestablishes some of the guidelines for life that somehow got lost in the modern era.

I am thankful that the heroes of the faith are rising again, with no thought for their own lives, living only for the purposes and glory of God. Years ago, I wrote this slogan to help me remember how to live life: "Fear no man, fear God only, and love not your life unto death." I think that approach rightly terrifies the powers of darkness because the people of God can actually live like the people of God, and transform the world for His glory.

Prayer

Dear heavenly Father, I look to You for help, as it would be easy for me to try to earn what was already purchased with the blood of Your Son, Jesus. Because of such a priceless gift, I am dissatisfied to live a life of mere convenience. I give myself to You today, and every following day, as a living sacrifice. My whole desire is for You to be glorified by what I can accomplish for Jesus in response to the price He paid. My God, be forever glorified!

Confession

It is my privilege to give everything for the glory of God. His sacrifice for me resets the standard of what love looks like. How can I not love Him in return? So I give myself as an offering, that He might be forever glorified!

77

Hope

If God is your servant, He will
always disappoint you. If you are
His servant, He will always surpass
your greatest expectations.

I have noticed in recent years that as the Church discovers her
purpose in the earth, a segment of her population is highly
driven to accomplish things to meet those expectations. Parts
of their teaching and practice are doable and worth considering. But there is a breakdown. People who are driven, working
hard to attain what they consider their rights in the Kingdom,
usually end up with much disappointment or disillusionment.
Either can be deadly.

I am so locked into memorizing and meditating on the promises of God that it can be said they have kept me sane and alive
at times. Having hope is what wakes me up in the morning. But
the moment I treat those promises as rights, I become a bit more
demanding. My destiny is no longer a journey into the promises
of God. Instead, it is taking possession of what is owed to me as
a child of God. Strangely, even I as write this, I recognize their
reasoning, because a child of God does have rights. And there

is a place for taking possession of what is promised. Perhaps it is the attitude of heart that disturbs me. You can tell people are more driven than directed any time things do not work as they thought, prayed or planned. Those who are driven start questioning what is wrong with the system. You are supposed to be able to do steps one through three and come up with the prescribed answer.

The Bible is not a math book or a chemistry book that allows you to follow a formula over and over again a thousand times and get the same result every time. If we were simply dealing with Kingdom principles, it would work that way. We are not. We are dealing with a relationship with the King, who is looking for certain traits and characteristics to be built into the makeup of His sons and daughters, who are being groomed to reign with Him. The relational component changes everything. Those driven by achievement goals, above relationship goals, will find themselves in a constant place of frustration. And if they are honest, they are frustrated with God. He is so disappointing when we want Him to work for us.

But when we are His servants, thankful for the chance to serve in His Kingdom, everything is different. Our outlooks are different. Every little blessing is a blessing indeed. Nothing is taken for granted. And not only that, we find this wonderful King actually taking us aside and telling us He considers us friends. Wow! An unimaginable outcome: the King of glory calling us His friends. Everything He does for us or through us is now a bonus. He never disappoints, as our expectations are to know Him more. And when things do not work as we prayed, planned for or expected, we draw near, knowing that being with Him is the only healing for such a wounded heart.

God responds to our cries. He serves us, as Jesus did with the towel over His arm to wash feet. But He remains the King of glory. When I grasp the privilege of serving in His courts, and now as a trusted friend, He never disappoints. No, He never disappoints.

Prayer

Dear Father and God, I love Your promises so much. They are my food. Hope springs up in my heart because of them. Please help me never to use them against You to get my way, but instead to use them for Your purposes to be accomplished in me. I pray these things that You might be glorified because of me as a friend of God.

Confession

I am a servant of the Most High God. And even though I am a child of God and friend of the King, I will forever serve Him in honor. I embrace the promises of God, not as personal rights, but as invitations to partnership, that His purposes might be accomplished in me. And this I do for the glory of God.

78

Love

When faith works through love, fear is silenced.

Faith and love are the two absolutes expected to flow from a believer's life. We cannot please God apart from faith (see Hebrews 11:6), and the greatest of these is love (see 1 Corinthians 13:13). Faith connects us to the power issue, and love represents the issue of character. Both power and character are needed to be fully effective in this life as God intended. They were never meant to be separated. They are the two legs we stand on. These are two sides of the same coin, as character is always to be the vehicle that power rides on.

And then we have the number-one command of Scripture, repeated more often than any other: Do not fear. It should not surprise us that the number-one tool of the powers of darkness is aimed at our supreme purpose, moving in love, displaying His power.

Fear cripples. We all know that. With it we lose our sense of balance, distorting how we walk. Fear usually starts with a bad idea that we take time to consider. Recognizing that such thoughts are illogical seldom helps in dealing with them, because fear is spiritual—fear is often a spirit. In other words, there is an evil presence involved, adding power to the fear so that as we agree with it, it might be able to kill, steal and destroy.

Fear confuses. The longer I listen to fear, the more confused I become over what God has promised for my life. If I fall into fear, I forget what God has taught me, I lose sight of the tools He has given me, and I no longer anticipate the destiny God has promised. It is not that I blame God; I know better than that. I just personalize the fear so much that I feel disqualified from the fullness of God's purposes in my life. In that frame of mind, I am likely to think that I am just not spiritual enough, or that I do not have enough faith.

Fear has a blinding effect. Oddly enough, I can even get to the place where I no longer remember much that God has done in my life. This tool is used to make me, a believer, feel inferior to the powers of darkness, when the opposite is true.

Fear can be successful only if it turns my attention from God toward myself or my problems. It is all downhill from there. But fear is easily defeated. "There is no fear in love; but perfect love casts out fear, because fear involves punishment, and the one who fears in not perfected in love" (1 John 4:18). The answer is found in the love of God. There are times when I stop praying for the things on my list, and stop singing the songs I love that bring Him honor, and stop all other obvious activities that have great value for the believer. In their places I do one thing: I sit in God's presence and say something like this: "I'm here, still, just for You to love me." Then I turn my affection toward Him and wait. He is such a lover that He is drawn to our stillness, our posture of focused inactivity.

Something happens when we take a different route than mentioned a few paragraphs earlier—when I will not entertain the devil's ideas, when I will not consider what could go wrong, when I will not feed myself on the fear of man, and I simply turn my heart to the God of my faith. When that happens, then I have caused the enemy of my soul great difficulties. Paul says to stand "in no way alarmed by your opponents—which is a sign of destruction for them, but of salvation for you, and that too, from God" (Philippians 1:28). My not being afraid reminds the devil he is doomed, finished and sentenced to eternal judgment, while having to live with the fact that I am one of the redeemed ones, saved by the precious blood of Jesus, with unlimited blessings from a loving God.

Not fearing has rewards for me and torment for the powers of darkness. I would be happy with either of those results. But having both of them is certainly a bonus!

Prayer

Heavenly Father, help me to recognize when the enemy is trying to pull me away from Your promises, and from Your presence. I commit myself to a faith that flows through love, that You might be forever exalted.

Confession

Both faith and love are in my nature as a child of God. I will resist the devil, knowing he will flee from me. He is terrified of me because of my place in the heart of God. I will live in faith, through love, for the glory of God.

79

Faith, Hope and Love

"For God so loved the world, that He gave His only begotten Son, that whoever believes in Him shall not perish, but have eternal life" *(John 3:16)*.

This is the quote of all quotes and the statement of all statements. It carries the heart of all I address in this book—faith, hope and love. These components are expressed beautifully in this one verse.

Love gives—the perfect Father gave us His Son. Faith receives the gift of the Father, His only Son. By believing in Jesus, we inherit eternal life and live forever in perfect harmony with God. Hope feeds on the promise of God both for now and eternal life. The provision of salvation for the body, soul and spirit has been given to us through Jesus. It is the Good News in its simplest form.

This verse profoundly reveals the heart of God, a loving Father. When we think of bringing heaven to earth through our prayers, it really starts with this theme: God loves people,

people respond to God, and whenever we respond to Him, His Kingdom is present.

This dominion of the Almighty is discovered through surrender. Our surrender is giving up on sin and death, and yielding to righteousness and life. It is being transferred from the kingdom of darkness to the Kingdom of light. This Kingdom has a Father, which means the entire function of the Kingdom is a family operation. Everything about it is healthy and progressive and has a future. But one thing cannot be forgotten: *God loved the world*, the *whole* world! This is not about gathering just a few lucky souls that have the chance to hear the Good News.

By implication, this verse also commissions, for how can we stay where we are after hearing that eternal life is for all who believe? We have been commissioned to do as Jesus did: Destroy the works of the devil, announce that the Kingdom of God is within arm's reach, and manifest what that Kingdom looks like when it touches the broken parts of life.

We do these things by remaining in love, always believing, and holding on to hope, regardless of circumstances. This beautiful privilege is given to all who believe. Eternal life affects this present life by the same means used to obtain eternal life: faith. Faith grows in the atmosphere of hope and is to be expressed through the vehicle of love.

Embrace the challenge, the invitation and the summons of God Almighty, our Father: Kingdom of God, *Come!*

Prayer

Wonderful heavenly Father, I receive the gift of Your Son, Jesus Christ, and rejoice in the salvation given to me. Help me always to be anchored in the hope of eternity. And help me always to demonstrate my faith through love. I purpose to live this way so that Your Kingdom will come and Your will be done on earth as in heaven. I pray these things that You might be forever glorified.

Confession

I love God with my whole heart, because He loved me first. My faith is in Jesus completely, for He is faithful. I live my life in such a way that His purposes are accomplished—on earth as it is in heaven. For it is my sole desire for God to be glorified in and through me.

Bill Johnson is senior pastor of Bethel Church in Redding, California. A fifth-generation pastor with a rich heritage in the power of the Spirit, he is the bestselling author of *When Heaven Invades Earth*. Bill and his wife, Beni, serve a growing number of churches through an apostolic network that has crossed denominational lines, partnering for revival. Bill and Beni live near Redding, California.

Essential Resources from Bill Johnson and Randy Clark

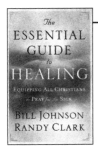

The ministry of healing is *not* reserved for a select few. In this practical, step-by-step guide, Bill Johnson and Randy Clark show how you, too, can become a powerful conduit of God's healing power.

The Essential Guide to Healing by Bill Johnson and Randy Clark

For the first time, Bill Johnson and Randy Clark candidly share their personal journeys behind life in the healing spotlight. With honesty, humor and humility, they recount the failures, breakthroughs and time-tested advice that propelled them into effective ministry.

Healing Unplugged by Bill Johnson and Randy Clark